BRAIN
POWER

BRAIN
POWER

UNLEASH THE POWER OF YOUR MIND

MICHAEL J. GELB
and KELLY HOWELL

Foreword by
TONY BUZAN

JAICO PUBLISHING HOUSE

Ahmedabad Bangalore Bhopal Bhubaneswar Chennai
Delhi Hyderabad Kolkata Lucknow Mumbai

Published by Jaico Publishing House
A-2 Jash Chambers, 7-A Sir Phirozshah Mehta Road
Fort, Mumbai - 400 001
jaicopub@jaicobooks.com
www.jaicobooks.com

First published in the United States of America by
New World Library
a division of Whatever Publishing Inc.
14 Pamaron Way, Novato, CA 94949, USA

To be sold only in India, Bangladesh, Bhutan,
Pakistan, Nepal, Sri Lanka and the Maldives.

BRAIN POWER
ISBN 978-93-88423-32-8

First Jaico Impression: 2019

Printed by
Thomson Press (India) Limited

If you are mindful that old age has wisdom for its food
you will so exert yourself in youth
that your old age will not lack sustenance.

— LEONARDO DA VINCI

Contents

BRAIN SYNC®: IMPROVE YOUR MIND AS YOU AGE

Accompanying this book is a complimentary brain wave training audio program designed to optimize mental performance. Instructions for downloading the audio files are in chapter 8 (page 165). The audio program contains four tracks:

- Track 1 provides a demonstration of how brain–wave audio technology balances your brain.
- Track 2 (*Pure Coherence*) refreshes your brain, clears mental fog, and focuses your mind like a laser beam. It also works as a natural antidepressant to boost your mood and energy levels. You'll feel alert and energized as your ability to think, concentrate, and store information is improved dramatically.
- Track 3 (*Deep Resonance*) allows you to effortlessly reach depths of meditation that would otherwise take years of practice to attain. As you listen, muscles relax, fears vanish, and stress fades; negative thoughts are washed away by streams of creative insight.
- Track 4 (*Slow-Wave Sleep*) encourages restful, regenerative sleep. With regular use of this track, you'll establish healthier sleep patterns and feel more refreshed in the morning.

Foreword

by Tony Buzan

The twenty-first century is the beginning of the Millennium of the Mind. In this new era, humanity will come to realize and apply the extraordinary power of the human brain. Over the past fifty years, I've devoted my life to helping create a world in which every child is raised with full knowledge of his or her astounding potential and how to utilize it. *Mental literacy* is the term I coined to refer to a practical understanding of every individual's capacity for information processing, memory development, creative thinking, problem solving, and continuous learning. The "king of literacies," it includes knowledge of the fundamentals of the physical structure and nature of the brain, and an understanding of the alphabet of the brain's behavioral repertoire.

About twenty years ago, during dinner, Ted Hughes, the former poet laureate of Great Britain, and I were discussing the benefits for humanity that will be realized when we fully unleash the great natural resource of human intelligence. In a moment of inspiration, we raised our glasses in a new toast to planetary mental literacy: "*Floreant dendritae!*" (a hybrid of ancient Greek and Latin meaning "May your brain cells flourish!").

Reading and applying the messages in *Brain Power: Improve Your Mind as You Age* will result in a remarkable flourishing of your one hundred billion brain cells. In this marvelous book, Michael J. Gelb and Kelly Howell make a profoundly valuable contribution to the field of mental literacy. Although there is considerable material on optimizing mental function as we age available on the Internet and in various publications, this book focuses in laser-like fashion on the most important, scientifically valid, and useful information on improving your mind as you age. It is immensely readable, easily accessible, and immediately applicable to every aspect of your life. *Brain Power* offers a practical program for increasing well-being now and for the rest of your life.

I know the value of the lessons in this book because I had the good fortune to have a mother who exemplified everything that Michael and Kelly recommend. My mom, Jean Buzan, was a tremendous inspiration to me and to just about everyone she ever met. Although she was a gifted student, Mom was forced at the age of sixteen, in 1932, to leave school. In those days, college wasn't an option for a girl from her background.

It was not until she was in her early fifties that she decided to go to college. With her feisty, positive attitude, she persuaded the authorities, first, that she was not "too old" to start a degree and, second, that she should skip the bachelor's degree and go straight into studying for a master's!

Mom had an advantage that helped her excel: she was mentally literate! An accomplished speed-reader and Mind Mapper, Mom was awarded her master's degree summa cum laude. What was her field? Gerontology! That is, the study of human beings as they age. For ten years, Mom lectured at the university on this subject, consistently making the point that you can get better in virtually all areas as you age. She was a living example of the material she was teaching.

Ironically — and displaying the outdated thinking about age that is still prevalent — her college insisted that she retire at the mandatory retirement age of sixty-five. "How ludicrous!" she exclaimed to me. "Just when I reach the age in which I'm applying everything I studied to get my degree, and have lectured on it for ten years, they decide that I am no longer qualified to teach it!" In happy rebellion, Mom printed business cards that proclaimed, "Jean M. Buzan, retired but inspired!" Mom continued writing, teaching, and inspiring others well into her nineties. As a gerontologist, Mom was devoted to overturning negative myths about aging.

One of the most common myths about aging is that memory inevitably declines. But I know from the growing body of scientific evidence and from witnessing Mom in action that this isn't necessarily true. In reality, your memory behaves much like your body in some very important ways. If you look after your body and nurture it, it remains flexible, resilient, and strong. If you neglect it, it becomes rigid, stagnant, and weak. The good thing about your memory is that it can improve every day of your life. Your memory is not like a container that fills up. It is a network of interlinked images and data that can grow infinitely as long as you continue to use it. The older you are, the greater and more powerful your memory can become.

Many people are concerned, however, that years of bad habits will prevent them from improving mental performance. In other words, they feel that it's "too late." But bad habits are simply neurological patterns that build up networks of probabilities by forming "memory traces" along the pathways between your brain cells. The more you repeat the behavior, the more these networks expand and the more the probability of your repeating the behavior increases. All you have to do, therefore, to reverse this trend is to establish new and more positive patterns of connection in your brain. By repeating these, you increase the probability that they will happen, and you decrease the probability that your old bad habits will persist. This book is a manual for the creation of new, more positive patterns of connection in your brain.

Your brain is astonishingly adaptable and flexible. You can continue to learn new skills and improve for as long as you live. Even if you've been doing the opposite of everything that Michael and Kelly teach in these pages, you'll still be able to turn things around and reap the benefits. I've been preaching the gospel of the flexible, adaptable brain since the late 1960s, and as you'll learn in this book, scientific research has now confirmed the idea that you can improve your mind as you age.

I first met Michael in 1975 when I was invited to lecture on the brain at the School for Alexander Technique Studies in London. After my presentation, I commented to the school's director that I was particularly impressed with the incisive questions asked by one of the students. Unbeknownst to me, Michael, the incisive questioner, had also approached the director to inquire as to how he might learn more about my work. Thus began a collaboration and friendship that continue to this day. In the late 1970s, we traveled the world together leading five-day mind and body seminars for senior managers. In 1982, Michael became the first person to be certified as a master trainer of my work, and since that time, he has evolved into one of the world's great original thought leaders in the fields of creative thinking, innovative leadership, and development of human potential.

And this book has another exceptional feature: the *Brain Sync: Improve Your Mind as You Age* download that accompanies this text provides an elegant way to "tune up" your brain and optimize mental performance. This easy-to-use audio program increases mental clarity, improves memory, and allows you to enjoy many of the same benefits experienced by long-term meditators. Understanding the nature of brain waves and how to synchronize them is an important element in the curriculum of mental literacy. And Kelly Howell, creator of Brain Sync audio technology, is the world's leading innovator in the practical application of brain wave research. Her outstanding meditation and brain optimization programs are used in hospitals and biofeed-back clinics, and by hundreds of thousands of individuals worldwide.

Together, Michael and Kelly provide you with the most valuable, life-changing knowledge and practices you can use to unleash your brain power and improve your mind as you age. *Floreant dendritae!*

INTRODUCTION

A Whole New Brain

Poised on a ladder under a pomegranate tree, Bill delights in picking the ripe fruit. As the sun sets behind the coastal mountains, the pines etched in gold, he exults, "What a glorious day!" In that moment, the early evening light seems to shine more brightly.

Bill is ninety. He's as trim as he was during World War II as a major in the U.S. Air Force. Some say he defied gravity — working with passion to build his own business from nothing while savoring every moment.

As a child growing up during the Depression, Bill served neighbors in the teahouse his mother created in their living room.

> *The brain is…*
> *the most complex thing*
> *we have yet discovered in our*
> *universe. It contains hundreds of*
> *billions of cells interlinked through*
> *trillions of connections. The brain*
> *boggles the mind.*
>
> — JAMES D. WATSON,
> Nobel laureate

1

Service is one of his core principles: service to neighbors, community, and country. Whether it's saying kind words to a stranger, mentoring his friends and children, or fund-raising for charities, when Bill talks about giving, his eyes light up as if he'd found the greatest secret of all. "There's nothing more rewarding than giving," he enthuses. "The rewards you get back are so much greater than what you give!"

Bill's mind is sharp. He excels at bridge and enjoys spirited debates about politics and social issues. He remembers names, faces, dates, and events with ease. Bill contends that remembering names and faces — an ability he developed years before when he took a memory-training course — was one of the keys to his success in the highly competitive automobile sales and service business. One thing Bill learned in his memory course was to bring his full attention when meeting someone for the first time. It doesn't matter if it's a waitress or a CEO; he's genuinely curious about people, and when he focuses on you, it's as though you're the most important person in the world.

Bill starts his day with twenty minutes of stretching, sit-ups, and weight training, and then a stroll with his dog, Biscuit. His mental exercise includes jotting down some of the things that make him feel grateful every day. He also reads biographies of great men and women and aims to apply their wisdom in his life.

Although he has some physical ailments, you'd never know it. He'd rather talk about the latest 49ers game than listen to people whine about their problems. "When the conversation starts going south," he says, "I change the subject."

When asked, "What's your secret?" Bill responds, "Curiosity!" He explains, "When I drove to and from work for decades on the same road, I always looked for something I hadn't noticed before — a new tree, a new fence, a new home. I still do that. Being aware of the small details is one of the ways I stay alert." Bill offers more sage advice: "Keep learning new things." "Whatever you do, stay connected to people." "Practice the Golden Rule." "Forgive." And, with a mischievous twinkle in his clear brown eyes, "A little flirting doesn't hurt either."

Bill practices, intuitively, much of what you will learn in the pages that follow.

The New Paradigm for Optimal Aging

Who are your role models for aging? What are your expectations and attitudes about the progress of your mind as you get older? Do you expect your memory to be better or worse in ten or twenty years? How about your sex life? What are your fears, concerns, and worries about getting older? Are you hoping that someone will develop the mental equivalent of Viagra?

Let go of the idea of "anti-aging." Resistance against getting older is futile. Instead, embrace the idea of aging well, with wisdom and poise.

In the past thirty years, the scientific evidence supporting the notion that your mind can improve through the years has become overwhelming. Clearly, the question is no longer *whether* your mind can improve with age but, rather, *how* you can optimize your mental powers as you get older.

This book presents practical, evidence-based wisdom to help you answer this question. You'll learn new skills to increase memory, intelligence, creativity, and concentration. And you'll cultivate greater confidence and healthy optimism as you discover how to improve your mind as you age.

We've interviewed leading experts, including physicians, gerontologists, and neuroscientists; and we've studied the practices of men and women who are paragons of healthy aging. Our approach isn't just based on scientific theory and academic research — we actually *apply* everything recommended in these pages. And we will guide you to do the same so that you can improve your mind every year of your life.

Over the past three decades, a paradigm shift has taken place in the field of neuroscience. This shift has shattered everything we once believed to be true about the aging brain.

Most of us were raised with faulty ideas about our mental capacity — such as the notion that IQ is fixed at age five, that brain cells degrade yearly after age thirty, and that memory and learning ability inevitably decline with age.

These notions, based on the scientific understanding that was prevalent in the 1950s, are myths — dangerous myths that can stifle our ability to flourish in the second half of life.

Just as Copernicus overturned the myth that the earth was at the center of the universe, so contemporary neuroscience has revolutionized our understanding of the potential to improve mental functioning as we age. We now know the following.

- *Your mental abilities, including memory, are designed to improve throughout life.* Neuroscientists call this neuroplasticity (neuro refers to neurons, otherwise known as brain cells, and plasticity is the quality of being changeable or malleable). As neuroscientist Richard Restak, MD, emphasizes, "Your brain is designed to improve with use."

- *Although some brain cells die as we age, we can generate new cells.* Neuroscientists call this *neurogenesis*. Gene Cohen, MD, PhD, director of the Center for Aging, Health and Humanities at George Washington University, states, "We can indeed form new brain cells, despite a century of being told that it's impossible." Your neuronal endowment is so great that even if you lost one thousand brain cells every day for the rest of your life, you would still only be losing less than 1 percent of your total. (Of course, it's important not to lose the 1 percent that you actually use!)

The brain is not, as was once thought, a compartmentalized, hardwired, static machine whose parts eventually wear out. Instead, it is a highly adaptable and dynamic organ, capable of generating new neurons and improving as we get older. People of average intelligence can, with appropriate training, raise their IQ, enhance their memory, and sharpen their intelligence throughout life.

We will reveal the evidence for this new paradigm and, most importantly, we will show you how to incorporate this new understanding into your life so that, like our friend Bill, you can improve your mind as you age.

THE BRAIN THAT CHANGES ITSELF

Neuroplasticity has been brought to public attention largely through the work of Norman Doidge, MD. In reviewing Doidge's book *The Brain That Changes Itself*, the *New York Times* states, "The power of positive thinking finally gains scientific credibility. Mind-bending, miracle-making, reality-busting stuff...with implications for all human beings, not to mention human culture, human learning and human history."

Unleashing Your Brain Power for a Synergy of Improvement

You are about to discover that the power of your brain is greater than anything you may have previously imagined. You possess an astounding instrument of intelligence, and you are on the verge of learning how to unleash its vast potential.

In 1941, Sir Charles Sherrington, the Nobel Prize—winning neurophysiologist, referred to the brain as an "enchanted loom" where "millions of flashing shuttles weave a dissolving pattern, always a meaningful pattern, though never an abiding one." Some twenty years later, Professor Pyotr Anokhin of Moscow State University focused on quantifying the complexity of the enchanted loom by calculating the number of possible thought patterns that the average human brain can make. He

If we did all the things we are capable of doing, we would literally astound ourselves.

— THOMAS EDISON

concluded that the number of connections is "virtually infinite." And, more recently, neuroscientist Marco Iacoboni, MD, PhD, of the Ahmanson-Lovelace Brain Mapping Center at UCLA explains, "The brain has an almost boundless capacity for reshaping itself over the years, for adapting, for expanding its power, while accumulating knowledge and recording experiences. Modern neuroscience tells us that the aging brain is no longer the declining brain, but rather a learning organ whose limits are still unexplored."

SCIENCE AND POETRY EXPRESS THE SAME UNDERSTANDING OF THE AWE-INSPIRING POWER OF THE HUMAN BRAIN

If the human brain were so simple that we could understand it, we would be so simple that we couldn't.

— Emerson Pugh, PhD,
in *The Biological Origin of Human Values*

The brain is wider than the sky,
For, put them side by side,
The one the other will include
With ease, and you beside.

The brain is deeper than the sea,
For, hold them, blue to blue,
The one the other will absorb,
As sponges, buckets do.

— Emily Dickinson

In this book, you'll discover how to weave the most positive, productive patterns within the infinite loom of your mind. You will activate unused areas of your brain, tone your mental muscles, and enliven all your faculties. And you'll be amazed to realize just how quickly you can generate positive results.

These techniques are presented in eight chapters, each highlighting an essential aspect of improving your mind as you age. Each chapter sets the stage for the subsequent chapters, and as you learn and practice, you'll discover that the benefits multiply. You'll find that this simple, systematic method creates a synergy of improvement.

Although you may be familiar with the idea that continuous learning, healthy diet, and regular exercise are important for cultivating your mind, we will guide you to apply the most reliable, helpful, and practical advice. And you'll learn things that may be completely new, such as the dramatic effect that attitude has on your longevity, how to use the techniques devised by the ancient Greeks to strengthen your memory, and how to balance your moods and emotions for optimal brain function.

Extensive research reveals that accumulated stress is the greatest cause of age-related mental and physical decline. This book includes a link to download a free *Brain Sync: Improve Your Mind as You Age* audio program designed to dissolve stress and optimize your mental performance. This easy-to-use audio technology is clinically proven to balance the right and left hemispheres of your brain, creating states of deep calm and high coherence — the same kind of coherence associated with the creativity of great minds like Leonardo da Vinci and Thomas Edison.

But is it really possible to change deep-seated habits? And isn't our potential limited by genetic predispositions? The debate about the influence of *nature* (our genetic endowment) versus the influence of *nurture* (the effects of our upbringing, environment, and education) has engaged scientists through the centuries. Although our genes do play a significant role in determining our capabilities, scientists now agree we can change our habits and develop our minds throughout life. In his book *Genome*, science writer Matt Ridley concludes, "Mother Nature has plainly not entrusted the determination of our intellectual capacities to the blind fate of a gene." And cell biologist Bruce H. Lipton, PhD, offers a more personal expression: "I was exhilarated by the new realization that I could change the character of my life by changing my beliefs. . . . I realized that there was a science-based path that would take me from my job as a perennial 'victim' to my new position as 'co-creator' of my destiny."

In the first century BCE, the Roman philosopher Seneca realized that we could change our lives by changing our beliefs; he advised that the process of aging "abounds with pleasure if you know how to use it." Bring more pleasure, fulfillment, and exhilaration to your life by using these proven techniques to improve your mind at any age.

CHAPTER ONE

Think Counterclockwise

S ome contend that age is a terrible price to pay for wisdom, but it needn't be, if we are mindful about our approach to aging. Surprising research reveals that opening our minds to what's possible, instead of presuming impossibility, can lead to a longer life, better health, and a stronger brain.

Since most of us were raised with the faulty notions that the brain deteriorates with age, that learning is easier when we are younger, and that memory loss is inevitable, we severely underestimate the power of a positive attitude. We also tend to overlook the hidden effects of cultural

Human beings, by changing the inner attitudes of their minds, can change the outer aspects of their lives.

— WILLIAM JAMES, American psychologist and philosopher

influences on our attitudes and beliefs about aging, influences that can drain mental and physical vitality from our lives.

Death may be nature's way of telling you to slow down. And some of our parts do wear out as we use them, but, fortunately, the brain isn't one of them.

Social psychologist Ellen J. Langer, PhD, has revolutionized our understanding of the relationship between attitude and aging. Langer's remarkable "counterclockwise" study demonstrates the astonishing power of a positive mind-set regarding our mental and physical health.

In 1979, Langer and her graduate students arranged for two groups of elderly men, who were in the care of relatives, to go on weeklong retreats at a secluded monastery in New Hampshire. Before attending their respective retreats, the men underwent a battery of tests measuring everything from intelligence to visual memory, dexterity, hearing, and vision.

The first group of men was invited to reminisce about life twenty years earlier, in 1959. At the end of the week, the group who reminisced reported that they had a pleasant week, and they showed some improvements in their mental and physical functioning when they were retested.

The second group was instructed to return as completely as possible in their minds to 1959. Every conversation was to be held in the present tense, and the men were instructed not to discuss anything that happened after September 1959. The experiment was meticulously staged with props and decor from the 1950s. At meals, the men engaged in heated debates on issues of the day such as the threat of communism, the need for bomb shelters, and Castro's advance into Havana. They shared thoughts on "recent" books such as Ian Flemings's *Goldfinger* and Philip Roth's *Goodbye, Columbus*. And they watched "newly released" movies such as *Ben-Hur* and *Some Like It Hot*. In the evenings, they enjoyed *Ed Sullivan*, *Sgt. Bilko*, and *Gunsmoke* on a black-and-white television set. Perry Como, Rosemary Clooney, and Nat King Cole sang on the phonograph. They listened to the radio as Royal Orbit won the Preakness, and they watched the Baltimore Colts defeat the New York Giants, 23–17, in the NFL championship game.

What happened? All the participants became more active. They started serving their own meals and cleaning up afterward, and they took the initiative to arrange their own social activities, such as card games and book discussion groups. Langer observed, "Despite their obvious and extreme dependence on relatives who initially drove them to Harvard's psychology department…they were all functioning independently almost immediately upon arrival at the retreat."

Follow-up tests at the end of the week revealed that participants showed dramatic improvements in memory, flexibility, vision, hearing, appetite, and general well-being. The most striking result from Langer's study is that, after the men lived as though they were younger for only one week, their shriveled, arthritic fingers actually lengthened and released as the men embraced a more youthful attitude.

How powerful is attitude? According to Langer, "Simply having a positive attitude made far more difference than any to be gained from lowering blood pressure or reducing cholesterol." She concludes, "While exercise and eating well are important for health, our attitudes about what it means to be healthy or to be old may be even more important."

When Langer's subjects returned in their minds to a time when they were younger and healthier, their brains underwent a radical change and literally grew younger. Langer suggests that if a group of elderly adults can produce such dramatic changes, perhaps the rest of us can make changes, too. "I have come to believe less and less that biology is destiny," she says. "It is not primarily our physical selves that limit us, but rather our mindset about our physical limits."

Your brain is plastic, adaptable, and capable of development throughout your life. Biology doesn't fully determine your destiny, and your limits are more self-imposed than inherited. Knowing that you *can* improve your brain is the beginning of improving it, because your attitude serves as a powerful self-fulfilling prophecy.

The Power of Expectations

How strong is the effect of mind-set on longevity? Langer's associate, Becca Levy, PhD, was determined to find out. Beginning in 1975, she surveyed 650 people about their expectations regarding the aging process. Subjects responded to statements such as "Things keep getting worse as I get older" or "I am as happy now as I was when I was younger."

Dr. Levy and her colleagues used the survey to categorize respondents as either negative or positive in their attitude toward aging. More than twenty years later, she discovered that the group with more positive, optimistic expectations about aging had outlived the more negative, pessimistic group by an average of more than seven years.

Commenting on Levy's research, neuroscientist Valerie Gremillion, PhD, says, "So this doesn't seem like magic, let's point out these effects can occur through a number of known mechanisms, from decreasing depression and increasing motivation, to psycho-neuroendocrine effects on the immune system, and through active engagement with the world and an associated decrease in feelings of loneliness and helplessness."

Consider this groundbreaking fact: by increasing awareness of the way you form attitudes and expectations about aging, you can influence the quality and duration of your life. With this in mind, let's begin cultivating the most adaptive attitudes for healthy aging.

> *Expectations determine outcomes. If you expect your mental and physical capacity to diminish with age, it probably will. If you have the expectation that you will grow younger and live longer, this will be your experience.*
>
> — DEEPAK CHOPRA, author of *Ageless Body, Timeless Mind*

Learn Optimism to Achieve Better Results

"Old age," said Bette Davis, "is not for sissies." Anyone can be optimistic when everything is going her way. If you are in perfect health and just fell in love, you don't get much credit for being optimistic. Optimism counts when you face difficulties. Resilience in the face of adversity is the most distinguishing characteristic of those who age gracefully and adapt well. And resilience is a function of optimism.

Martin E. P. Seligman, PhD, pioneer of positive psychology and author of *Learned Optimism*, followed the development of optimists and pessimists over the course of decades. Seligman discovered that optimists get better results than pessimists in most areas of life: optimists outperform on their aptitude tests, get sick less frequently, recover faster when they do get ill, and make significantly more money. (The pessimists who are reading this are getting really depressed!) Seligman found that optimists get better results even though pessimists are better at accurately assessing the challenges and difficulties in a given situation.

The good news for pessimists is that an optimistic attitude can be developed. The key is what Seligman calls "explanatory style." In other words, pessimists and optimists tend to have very different self-coaching strategies in the face of adversity, and pessimists can learn the more adaptive and creative approach that leads optimists to achieve better results. Seligman expresses it this way: "The defining characteristic of pessimists is that they tend to believe that bad events will last a long time, will undermine everything they do, and are their own fault. The optimists, who are confronted with the same hard knocks of this world, think about misfortune in the opposite way. They tend to believe that defeat is just a temporary setback or a challenge, that its causes are just confined to this one case."

No pessimist ever discovered the secret of the stars, or sailed to an uncharted land, or opened a new doorway for the human spirit.

— HELEN KELLER

So if a pessimist experiences an age-related disorder,

such as degenerative osteoarthritis of the hip that is so bad it requires a total hip replacement, the pessimist's internal dialogue might include phrases like these: "I will never be able to do what I used to do," "This will ruin everything," and "This is my fault for doing all that cross-country running when I was younger." The optimist approaches the same challenging circumstances with an internal dialogue that might include phrases such as these: "This surgery will allow me to do what I love to do again," "I will make the most of this temporary setback," "I will use the downtime to strengthen my patience and compassion, and will emerge as a wiser, more balanced person," and "I'm glad I conditioned my body to meet athletic challenges when I was younger, because I can use that experience to recover quickly and fully."

If a pessimist gives a presentation at work with the intention of gaining approval for a new project and the proposal is rejected, the pessimist's internal dialogue might include phrases like these: "My proposal isn't good enough, and I'm a failure," "This is a disaster — it makes a mockery of everything I've worked on," and "The situation is hopeless and will never change." The optimist approaches the same type of rejection with an internal dialogue that might include phrases such as these: "The board that rejected my proposal will have three new members in six months, so I will try again at that time," "I will use this time to strengthen my proposal so that it will be much more compelling and irresistible," and "I'm grateful for the opportunity to learn from this rejection — it will help me become more effective."

Optimists get better results in most areas of life because they stay engaged and continue to search for solutions. Pessimists assume that solutions aren't possible, so they stop seeking. Optimism is a skill of emotional intelligence that can be learned. The key is to become aware of your habitual internal dialogue so that you can then consciously embrace the most creative, resilient perspective on any challenge you face.

Pessimism leads to weakness, optimism to power.

— WILLIAM JAMES

Rewire Your Brain for Resilience and Brilliance

A primary tenet of neuroscience, formulated by Donald O. Hebb, PhD, is "Neurons that fire together wire together." Habits are formed from neuronal connections that, over time, get wired together in the brain. Many habits are useful, such as tying your shoes or flossing your teeth. But some habits, like worrying and other pessimistic thought patterns, aren't constructive and require conscious intervention to change.

Extreme habit patterns are observable in individuals who suffer from obsessive-compulsive disorder (OCD). OCD is characterized by repetitive behaviors and uncontrollable thoughts. Many OCD sufferers know that their ritualized behaviors, such as repetitive hand washing or checking the oven countless times to be sure that it's really off, are irrational, but the automatic pattern is so powerful they feel powerless to stop it.

Jeffrey M. Schwartz, MD, coauthor of *The Mind and the Brain: Neuroplasticity and the Power of Mental Force*, has been successfully teaching patients with severe OCD to rewire their brains in order to free themselves from destructive patterns of habitual thought and action. Schwartz's approach can be applied to rewiring any habitual pattern, including pessimistic thinking, even if you don't have OCD.

He counsels that you begin by observing the process of your mind at work. Acknowledge when worrisome, pessimistic, or anxiety-driven thoughts arise, and label them as by-products stemming from maladaptive wiring in your brain.

As you note the anxiety-producing thought pattern, you disconnect it from association with events in the external world and instead attribute it to the habitual circuitry in your brain, circuitry that you are now in the process of rewiring.

Dr. Schwartz advises that once you've become aware of a negative thought pattern, you should consciously alter the pattern of association by redirecting your attention to something pleasurable, such as listening to your favorite music, working in the garden, or playing with your pet. Even though you might be feeling anxiety or dread, you change the pattern of association in your brain as you willfully focus on something

In the central place of every heart there is a recording chamber. So long as it receives a message of beauty, hope, cheer, and courage — so long are you young. When the wires are all down and your heart is covered with the snow of pessimism and the ice of cynicism, then, and only then, are you grown old.

— GENERAL DOUGLAS MACARTHUR

pleasurable. With practice, this positive refocusing gradually rewires your negative neural circuitry.

Another method for mindfully changing pessimistic patterns and negative associations is "the Work," developed by Byron Katie, author of *Loving What Is*. In a process similar to the one developed by Dr. Schwartz, Katie teaches you to identify and question thoughts that cause suffering and then turn them around.

An unquestioned mind is the world of suffering.

— BYRON KATIE

For example, your negative thought might be, "I'm always forgetting things; my memory is getting worse with age." Katie counsels asking these four questions about the negative thought:

1. *Is it true?* Are you really *always* forgetting things? Do you ever remember anything?
2. *Can you absolutely know that it's true?* Absolute knowledge is elusive.
3. *How do you react — what happens — when you believe that thought?* Bring your attention to the physical reactions you have when you experience a pessimistic thought. What happens to your posture, your breathing, etc.?
4. *Who would you be without that thought?* This question invites you to let go of your attachment to the negative thought.

Katie suggests that, after you have investigated your statement with the four questions, you aim to experience the opposite of your original statement. She calls this a "turnaround." You might turn around the original statement ("I'm always forgetting things; my memory is getting worse with age") by stating, "I always remember important things. My ability to remember what's important is improving with age." Or, "I'm skilled at forgetting unimportant things. This improves the quality of my life as I get older."

As you learn to turn around your negative, pessimistic thought patterns, you'll feel better and respond to life's challenges in a more adaptive and creative manner.

Develop Mental Acuity and Extend Your Life with a Daily Dose of GFH

GFH isn't the latest hormone therapy. It's an acronym for three essential practices that improve mental acuity and extend your life: *gratitude*, *forgiveness*, and *humor*.

Age Gracefully with Gratitude

Gratitude has been lauded by many remarkable thinkers throughout history. For Thomas Jefferson, "the disposition to be grateful" was an essential key to happiness. The great physician, humanitarian, and Nobel laureate Albert Schweitzer explained, "The greatest thing is to give thanks for everything. He who has learned this knows what it means to live." And the Roman philosopher Cicero noted, "Gratitude is not only the greatest of the virtues but the parent of all others."

> *He is a wise man who does not grieve for the things which he has not, but rejoices for those which he has.*
>
> — EPICTETUS, Greek philosopher

The word *gratitude* comes from the Latin root *gratia*, translated as "grace." All major spiritual traditions emphasize the importance of grace and gratitude, but it is only in the past ten years or so that science has begun to validate what religion has always taught. Robert A. Emmons, PhD, Michael E. McCullough, PhD, and their colleagues have, as part of the Research Project on Gratitude and Thankfulness, conducted many experiments to measure the effects of the disposition to be grateful.

They discovered that people who count their blessings rather than their burdens are more adaptive, are more optimistic, and report a significantly greater experience of well-being. They write, "In an experimental comparison, those who kept gratitude journals reported fewer physical symptoms, felt better about their lives as a whole, and were more optimistic about the upcoming week compared to those who recorded hassles or neutral life events."

An attitude of gratitude is relatively easy to cultivate, and a simple gratitude journal is the best way to get started. Take a few minutes every morning to write out a list of things that inspire you to feel grateful. After you compose your list, spend a few seconds focusing on the feeling of gratitude for each thing you've written down. After you've reviewed your list, just "float" in the feeling of gratitude for a minute or so. Repeat the process in the evening. That's all it takes to get your immune system revved up. Practice this simple gratitude exercise, and you'll discover more grace in your everyday life. The British poet and philosopher G. K. Chesterton expressed it this way: "You say grace before meals. All right. But I say grace before the concert and the opera, and grace before the play and pantomime, and grace before I open a book, and grace before sketching, painting, swimming, fencing, boxing, walking, playing, dancing, and grace before I dip the pen in the ink." Rabbi Harold Kushner, author of *When Bad Things Happen to Good People*, also reminds us to appreciate the holiness of the everyday phenomena that we often take for granted. Like Chesterton, he recommends focusing attention on gratitude for simple things — the air you breathe or the clothes you wear. As you count your blessings, you discover that you are blessed.

The Economy of Forgiveness

The British poet and playwright Hannah Moore referred to forgiveness as the "economy of the heart." She explained, "It saves the expense of anger, the cost of hatred, the waste of spirits."

Along with gratitude, all the world's spiritual traditions also emphasize the importance of forgiveness. For many people, however, forgiveness is a more challenging attitude to embrace. As the great English poet Alexander Pope noted, "To err is human, to forgive divine." Not surprisingly, contemporary science has begun to demonstrate the benefits of this divine attribute.

Life is an adventure in forgiveness.

— NORMAN COUSINS

The practice of forgiveness boosts the immune system, lowers high blood pressure, reduces anxiety and depression, and improves sleep patterns, according to Fred Luskin, PhD, director of the Forgiveness Project at Stanford University and author of *Forgive for Good*. And Dr. Luskin's research suggests that forgiveness is a skill that can be learned. Developing your skill in forgiveness is easier when you remember the following points.

- *Forgiveness is for you.* Forgiveness is a powerful form of self-healing. It's important to learn to let go of toxic emotions because bitterness and resentment are physiologically harmful to the person who harbors them. Forgiveness is something you can do primarily for your own benefit. Holding a grudge drains your energy and compromises your well-being. In *The HeartMath Solution*, Doc Childre and Howard Martin explain, "Forgiving releases you from the punishment of a self-made prison in which you're both the inmate and the jailer."

- *Forgiveness strengthens your character.* Forgiving others, and yourself, liberates you from emotions that disrupt your peace of mind. As you take more responsibility for your internal experience and choose happiness over resentment, you affirm your inner strength and freedom. Gandhi reminds us, "The weak can never forgive. Forgiveness is the attribute of the strong."

- *Forgiveness isn't condoning.* In the movie *Unforgiven*, Bill (played by Gene Hackman) protests that he doesn't deserve to die and Munny (played by Clint Eastwood) responds, "Deserve's got nothin' to do with it." The same thing is true with forgiveness. And forgiving someone doesn't mean that you condone or excuse unacceptable behavior. You can strongly disapprove of another person's actions and still forgive him. You don't have to reconcile with someone or continue a relationship in order to forgive completely.

- *Forgiveness is the best revenge.* The inability to forgive is based on a flawed assumption: we mistakenly believe that anger and resentment can defend us against hurt feelings. But negative emotions don't protect us; they actually harm us, by unleashing a flood of stress hormones. So let go of the investment in this faulty strategy and focus instead on living as well as you can. And if you need a little mustard with your forgiveness, remember the words of Oscar Wilde, who quipped that you should always forgive your enemies because nothing annoys them more.

- *Forgiveness takes patience.* Learning to forgive takes practice and patience. Deep wounds and hurt feelings can be tenacious. Sometimes when we think we have forgiven and moved on, something happens to remind us of a past hurt, and we find ourselves consumed by it again. When this occurs, just notice the hurt feelings and, instead of judging yourself, renew your intention to let them go.

- *Forgiveness is easier with empathy.* It's much easier to forgive when we understand and empathize with the person we are forgiving. As the poet Henry Wadsworth Longfellow explained, "If we could read the secret history of our enemies, we would find in each person's life sorrow and suffering enough to disarm all hostility."

- *Forgiveness is easier with blessing.* You don't need to be religious or spiritual to bless someone. You can do it just because it will help you feel better. Pierre Pradervand, author of *The Gentle Art of Blessing*, describes a blessing as genuinely wishing the best for another person. He suggests that we "systematically replace every single thought of judgment with blessing — especially for that fellow at the office who drives you out of your wits!"

Just as blaming and resenting others weakens us, blessing them can provide a surprising source of strength. And you may be delighted to discover that your life becomes more harmonious as the blessings you give are returned to you.

Awaken More Brain Cells with Humor

In his classic book *Anatomy of an Illness as Perceived by the Patient*, Norman Cousins shares the story of his recovery from a form of severe degenerative arthritis. His most successful therapy was laughter. He watched silly movies and surrounded himself with mirth. "I made the joyous discovery that 10 minutes of genuine belly laughter had an anesthetic effect," he wrote.

Frame your mind to mirth and merriment, which bar a thousand harms and lengthen life.

— SHAKESPEARE

Many subsequent studies have proven Cousins right, showing that laughter has an analgesic effect (most likely because it releases endorphins into the bloodstream), especially for chronic pain from arthritis or neurological diseases. Laughter also eases muscle tension and suppresses the release of cortisol, the stress hormone. A 2001 study reported in the *Journal of the American Medical Association* showed that symptoms improved in allergy patients who viewed comedic movies, but not in those in the control group, who watched weather reports. Laughter boosts immunity and also "increases our heart rate, helps us breathe more deeply, and stretches many different muscles in our face and upper body," according to research by Richard Wiseman, PhD. "In fact," he adds, "it is like a mini workout."

Along with gratitude and forgiveness, humor is one of the most important attitudes for strengthening our well-being as we get older. Here are a few simple ways to add more laughter to your day.

> *When I was young, I was called a rugged individualist. When I was in my fifties, I was considered eccentric. Here I am doing and saying the same things I did then and I'm labeled senile.*
>
> — GEORGE BURNS, in the film *Just You and Me, Kid*

- Post a funny photo of yourself on your bathroom mirror as a reminder to avoid taking yourself too seriously.
- Keep a humor diary. Record your favorite jokes and funny stories, and share them with your friends. (Here's one: Two vultures board an airplane, each carrying two dead raccoons. The stewardess looks at them and says, "I'm sorry, gentlemen, only one carrion allowed per passenger.")

- Surround yourself with laughter. Invite friends over for an evening of joke telling (give a prize for the funniest), post your favorite cartoons in your office, or have a comedy movie evening.
- Smile and laugh for no reason. The great psychological pioneer William James explained, "We don't laugh because we are happy. We are happy because we laugh." James's assertion is supported by contemporary research. Paul Ekman, PhD, and his associates have demonstrated that smiling improves mood and positively influences the mood of others.
- Spend time with children and with family and friends who make you chuckle.
- Delight in puns. Punning is playful mental exercise. Although studies have yet to be conducted on the specific brain benefits, you will discover that a clever pun is its own *reword*. Is punning the lowest form of humor? Perhaps not: after all, limericks are verse.
- Luxuriate in nonsense. Make funny faces and sounds. Watch Monty Python's classic episode featuring the Ministry of Silly Walks and practice your own. As the legendary children's book author Dr. Seuss explains, "I like nonsense; it wakes up the brain cells."

The Language of Longevity

Language is powerful. The way you speak can reinforce or transform negative attitudes and stereotypes about aging. In the United States, negative stereotypes related to aging are everywhere; advertisements of all kinds tend to glorify youth and denigrate the elderly. We can, without knowing it, begin to internalize these negative stereotypes and inadvertently reinforce them by the way we use language.

In a study that demonstrates the power of words to reinforce or change negative stereotypes, Becca Levy, PhD, exposed different groups of older individuals to words flashed on a computer screen so quickly that they weren't consciously aware of what they were seeing. One group was exposed to words that reflect a positive attitude toward aging, such as *wisdom, experience,* and *creativity*. The other group was exposed to words that reflect a negative stereotype of aging, such as *disease, senile,* and *dying*. The group exposed to the negative words scored significantly lower on memory and mathematics tests, due to the increase in their stress levels and a decreased sense of self-confidence. According to a study by Dr. Levy and her colleagues, "Negative stereotypes of aging may contribute to health problems in the elderly without their awareness. This, in turn, could lead to older individuals mistakenly attributing a decline in their health to the inevitability of aging, which might then reinforce the negative stereotypes and prevent successful aging."

In other words, one's attitude toward aging serves as a self-fulfilling prophecy, for better or worse. This is compounded by the fact that language reinforces attitude. In

> *Words are, of course, the most powerful drug used by mankind.*
>
> — RUDYARD KIPLING

other studies, Dr. Levy and her colleagues have demonstrated that elderly participants exposed to words that reflect a positive attitude toward aging showed improvements in cardiovascular functioning, hearing, and even physical balance. They also found that in cultures that esteem aging, like Chinese culture, performance on memory tests tends to be higher among the elderly than it is in the more youth-worshipping United States.

FROM RETIREMENT TO RENAISSANCE

Derived from the French re- (back) and tirer (draw), retire means to "draw back." Clearly, this word has its drawbacks. Ernest Hemingway called it "the ugliest word in the language." When we consider a list of similar words — relinquish, surrender, separate, withdraw, regress, rescind, retreat — it seems that Hemingway may have a point. In any case, it's important to craft a positive, purposeful plan for a personal renaissance if you decide to transition away from a job or career. This is a great time to experience a rebirth of your passion for learning. As Seneca, the Roman philosopher, observed two thousand years ago, "Retirement without the love of learning is a living burial."

So be wary of conversations that focus on commiseration (literally "to be miserable together"). As Martha Graham warned, "Misery is a communicable disease." If you find yourself indulging in discussions that focus on how "things ain't what they used to be," shift to an emphasis on gratitude and appreciation. Savor the present moment and envision the future you wish to create.

FROM GEEZERS TO SAGES

In the United States, we tend to refer to older people in derogatory terms, such as

- Geezers
- Codgers
- Seniors
- Fogeys
- Geriatrics
- Curmudgeons
- Gramps/Granny

In other cultures, such as the Chinese and Native American, older people are considered in terms that are much more positive, even reverential, such as

- Sages
- The wise
- Elders
- Seers
- Patriarchs/Matriarchs
- Grandfather/Grandmother

If you adopt these more positive, life-affirming terms, you will strengthen your own self-concept as you age.

TOP TEN SELF-LIMITING PHRASES

Here are ten phrases that serve to reinforce negative stereotypes of aging:

- I'm having a senior moment.
- I'm not what I used to be.
- I'm too old.
- I can't remember anything anymore.
- My memory is going.
- Getting older stinks.
- Everything was easier when I was younger.
- I'm over the hill.
- My best days are behind me.
- Things keep getting worse as I get older.

Overcome Negative Stereotypes by Focusing on Inspiring Role Models

In the 1950s, marketers developed the strategy of planned obsolescence. A range of products, from automobiles to television sets, were designed so that they would fall apart shortly after the expiration of the warranty. Planned obsolescence became less viable as business competition became more global and communication technology increased consumer awareness. Unfortunately, the notion of planned obsolescence has maintained its grip on the American psyche in regard to our view of human beings.

As a graduate of the Zsa Zsa Gabor School of Creative Mathematics, I honestly do not know how old I am.

— ERMA BOMBECK

George Gerbner, PhD, former dean of the Annenberg School for Communication at the University of Pennsylvania, was a pioneer in documenting the extent of negative and prejudicial images of the elderly in the media. Author of many books and research papers, such as "The Image of the Elderly in Prime-Time Television Drama," Dr. Gerbner and his colleagues helped to raise awareness of how older people are negatively stereotyped or simply ignored.

Although Americans over seventy constitute more than 10 percent of the population, fewer than 3 percent of the characters portrayed on prime-time television are seventy or older. Dr. Gerbner and those who have followed in his footsteps have documented a disproportionate tendency for the media to portray seniors as senile, foolish, forgetful, and infirm. He commented, "Mass media, particularly television ...[have] a profound effect on the way we are socialized into our roles, including age as a social role."

A comprehensive review of studies on the portrayal of the elderly in the media, published in *Educational Gerontology*, concluded, "Negative stereotyping of the elderly circumscribes their potential by placing emphasis on the unproductive and unsuccessful older person and may become a self-fulfilling prophecy limiting capacities and experiences of aged persons. Negative stereotyping and ageism not only affect the elderly but also create negative expectations, fear, and dread of aging in the young."

Older people usually appear only in advertisements for pharmaceuticals, old-age homes, and devices to cope with infirmity ("I've fallen, and I can't get up"). As Dave Barry observes, the advertising industry "goes out of its way to make aging appear to be as attractive a process as death by maggot." He notes, "When you see older people in advertisements, they're usually having demeaning conversations with relentlessly cheerful pharmacists." Images of healthy, vital, active, sexy, wise, lively, and attractive older people are rare.

THE ART OF AGING

Alice and Richard Matzkin have applied their exceptional talents in painting and sculpture to create inspiring images of healthy aging. The Matzkins' art evokes the emergence of the soul through the years and serves as nourishment for a more positive image of the later phases of life. Their exquisitely illustrated book is entitled *The Art of Aging: Celebrating the Authentic Aging Self*, and their website (http://matzkinstudio.com) includes many beautiful images of older people.

Aging well is the supreme expression of wisdom. If you want to age well, nurture your wisdom by studying the lives of great men and women from all walks of life who continued to be productive and fulfilled in their later years. Make a conscious effort to focus on positive images of aging. Seek out older people who are vital and who can serve as inspiring role models.

"NOSTALGIA ISN'T WHAT IT USED TO BE"

Rudy is eighty-five. He had a stroke seven years ago but has recovered fully. Shortly after the stroke, Rudy and his wife of sixty years decided to move out of their home and into an "active retirement community." Although they initially had severe reservations about moving into such a facility, they've discovered that it's a blessing. Rudy works out at the gym three times a week, plays table tennis, runs the wine-tasting club, and is the baritone soloist in the choir. An avid reader, he usually has three or four books next to his favorite chair. While waiting in a long line for more than an hour, he quipped, "Most people my age would've forgotten what they were waiting in line for by now."

Rudy and his wife enjoy dining with their friends most evenings. Their dining group has a simple rule, "No whining!" or as one member phrased it, "No organ recitals." Their conversations usually focus on current events, movies, and book discussions; they don't spend much time reminiscing. As Rudy explains, "Nostalgia isn't what it used to be."

Although the members of their dining group have overcome a range of serious ailments, from cancer to heart disease, they are all in good health now, and they embody a positive, joyful, and grateful attitude toward life. Spending time with Rudy, his wife, and their friends is inspiring. They are informed, funny, and incisive as well as compassionate, kind, and wise.

The following are some examples of great role models for brilliant aging.

Michelangelo Buonarroti (1475–1564)

In 1530, at age fifty-five, Michelangelo designed the magnificent Laurentian Library in Florence. He began work as the architect of St. Peter's Basilica in Rome at the age of sixty-three and wrote in his journal during this time, "I am still learning." He also noted, "Genius is eternal patience."

John Adams (1735–1826) and Thomas Jefferson (1743–1826)

Adams and Jefferson served as the second and third presidents of the United States, respectively. These Founding Fathers dedicated their lives to the establishment of a new nation based on life, liberty, and the pursuit of happiness. They continued to be active thought leaders until they died, on the same day, July 4, 1826, exactly fifty years after signing the Declaration of Independence. Adams observed, "Old minds are like old horses; you must exercise them if you wish to keep them in working order." And Jefferson remarked, "Nothing can stop the man with the right mental attitude from achieving his goal; nothing on earth can help the man with the wrong mental attitude."

Johann Wolfgang von Goethe (1749–1832)

The great German poet and scientist completed part 2 of *Faust* (and there are only two parts) during the year of his death. Goethe scholar Raymond Keene calls it his "deepest and richest work." Goethe proposed, "We must always change, renew, rejuvenate ourselves; otherwise we harden."

Ludwig van Beethoven (1770–1827)

Despite the loss of his hearing, Beethoven continued to compose, conduct, and perform until he died. One of his greatest works, the Ninth Symphony, was his last. He proclaimed, "It seemed unthinkable for me to leave the world forever before I had produced all that I felt called upon to produce." And he advised, "Let us all do what is right, strive with all our might toward the unattainable, develop as fully as we can the gifts God has given us, and never stop learning."

Florence Nightingale (1820–1910)

Florence Nightingale became a legendary figure for her heroic and pioneering work caring for sick and wounded soldiers during the Crimean War. The godmother of the modern profession of nursing, she published her classic *Notes on Nursing* in 1859 and shortly thereafter (1860) established the world's first secular nursing school at St. Thomas' Hospital in London. Nightingale spent the next fifty years working to promote and organize the profession of nursing internationally. A gifted mathematician and an expert in statistical graphics, she stated, "I attribute my success to this — I never gave or took any excuse."

Harriet Tubman (1820–1913)

Harriet Tubman is a true American heroine. After escaping slavery, she devoted her life to liberating others and helped to create the Underground Railroad. In her later years, she also took on the cause of women's rights. "Every great dream begins with a dreamer," Tubman declared. "Always remember, you have within you the strength, the patience, and the passion to reach for the stars to change the world."

Helen Keller (1880–1968)

The first deaf-blind person to earn a bachelor's degree, Helen Keller was an author and champion of human rights and human potential. Well into her eighth decade, she worked with tireless devotion to raise funds for the American Foundation for the Blind. She was awarded the Presidential Medal of Freedom by President Lyndon Johnson in 1964 and was elected to the National Women's Hall of Fame in 1965. Keller observed, "As selfishness and complaint pervert the mind, so love with its joy clears and sharpens the vision."

Georgia O'Keeffe (1887–1986)

Despite progressive blindness, the pioneering artist continued to work until her death at age ninety-eight. In her later years, she blossomed as a landscape painter. She stated, "I decided to start anew, to strip away what I had been taught."

Edward L. Bernays (1891–1995)

Bernays coined the term *public relations* in 1919 and effectively invented the field. *Life* magazine named him one of the hundred most influential Americans of the twentieth century. When he turned one hundred, he said his mental age was "no different when I was 45." He added, "When you reach 100 don't let it throw you, because a person has many ages, and chronological is the least important."

Martha Graham (1894–1991)

Lauded as the dancer of the century by *Time* magazine in 1998, Graham was also included in the list of *Time*'s most important people of the twentieth century. Graham experienced a period of severe depression after she stopped dancing, but at the age of seventy-eight, she rallied and re-formed her dance company. In her remaining years, she choreographed ten major new works, including the "Maple Leaf Rag," completed one year before her death. "'Age' is the acceptance of a term of years," Graham believed. "But maturity is the glory of years." She also shared one of the great thoughts about creativity and individuality: "There is a vitality, a life force, an energy, a quickening that is translated through you into action, and because there is only one of you in all of time, this expression is unique."

George Burns (1896–1996)

The great comedian was also the bestselling author of ten books, including *How to Live to Be 100 — or More*. He continued making films and doing stand-up throughout his life, and he made the most of his age with lines such as "When I was a boy, the Dead Sea was only sick" and "How can I die? I'm booked." In a rare serious reflection, he observed, "How beautifully leaves grow old. How full of light and color are their last days."

Leroy Robert "Satchel" Paige (1906–1982)

Paige overcame racial discrimination to break into major-league baseball as a pitcher at the age of forty-two. He was elected to the Baseball Hall of Fame in 1971. When asked about his prowess at an age when most players are long retired, Paige responded by asking, "How old would you be if you didn't know how old you was?"

Grace Murray Hopper (1906–1992)

Rear Admiral Grace Murray Hopper ("Amazing Grace") was one of the first genius computer scientists. A pioneer in the development of COBOL, one of the original computer programming languages, she is also renowned for introducing the term *debugging* into the lexicon (the legend is that she created this neologism after removing a dead moth from a computer). An inspiring, effective, and innovative leader, she stated, "Humans are allergic to change. They love to say, 'We've always done it this way.' I try to fight that. That's why I have a clock on my wall that runs counterclockwise."

Peter Drucker (1909–2005)

The pioneering management guru continued to be an active thought leader, role model, and inspiration until the end. "We now accept the fact that learning is a lifelong process of keeping abreast of change," he said. "And the most pressing task is to teach people how to learn."

John Wooden (1910–2010)

The most successful collegiate men's basketball coach ever, Wooden is a member of the Basketball Hall of Fame. "It's what you learn after you know it all that counts," Wooden advised. He also remarked that "things turn out best for the people who make the best of the way things turn out."

Julia Child (1912–2004)

The legendary chef, author, and television star introduced fine French cuisine to the American public. When asked her advice on aging well, she responded, "Find something you're passionate about and keep tremendously interested in it." She also confided that her personal formula for longevity included plenty of "red meat and gin."

Rosalyn Yalow (1921–)

The medical physicist became the first woman to win a Lasker Award in 1976 and won the Nobel Prize for Medicine in 1977. "The excitement of learning separates youth from old age," Yalow affirms. "As long as you're learning you're not old."

Louise Hay (1926–)

The author of the global bestseller *You Can Heal Your Life*, Hay is an inspiring presence and the founder of the acclaimed Hay House publishing company. At age eighty-four, she reminds us, "Know that you are the perfect age. Each year is special and precious, for you shall only live it once. Be comfortable with growing older."

Murray Gell-Mann (1929–)

Winner of the Nobel Prize in Physics (1969), Murray Gell-Mann is a unique intellectual powerhouse. A passionate student of linguistics, cultural evolution, archeology, history, and the psychology of creative thinking, Gell-Mann is the prime mover of the renowned think tank at the Santa Fe Institute. At eighty-two, Gell-Mann is intensely curious and savors fine wine and fine cuisine. At a recent dinner in Santa Fe, he commented, "I think we all have the potential for genius. It's just a matter of discovering it."

Warren Buffett (1930–)

One of the richest men and greatest philanthropists of all time, Buffett is renowned as the "Sage of Omaha." In his early eighties, he continues to share his unparalleled insights into the art of investing, as chairman of Berkshire Hathaway, one of the largest public companies in the world. "Chains of habit are too light to be felt until they are too heavy to be broken," Buffett muses.

Clint Eastwood (1930–)

Eastwood began a new career as a director at age sixty-two with *Unforgiven* and has won two Academy Awards for best picture. At age seventy-eight, he became the oldest leading man in a number one box office hit, *Gran Torino*. Eastwood explains, "I'd like to be a bigger and more knowledgeable person ten years from now than I am today. I think that, for all of us, as we grow older, we must discipline ourselves to continue expanding, broadening, learning, keeping our minds active and open."

Sophia Loren (1934–)

The Oscar-winning actress and screen legend posed for the risqué Pirelli Calendar at age seventy-two along with much younger actresses such as Penélope Cruz and Hilary Swank. She remarks, "Beauty is how you feel inside, and it reflects in your eyes. It is not something physical." And she adds, "There is a fountain of youth: it is your mind, your talents, the creativity you bring to your life and the lives of people you love."

FIX YOUR COURSE TO A STAR

All of our positive role models have one element in common — their lives are organized around a powerful sense of purpose. Leonardo da Vinci advised his students, "Fix your course to a star and you can navigate through any storm." This was the maestro's way of emphasizing the importance of a guiding purpose in life. The German philosopher Nietzsche counseled, "Forgetting one's purpose is the commonest form of stupidity!" A guiding purpose, such as creating art or caring for others, is a major driver of healthy longevity.

Patricia A. Boyle, PhD, of Rush University Medical Center in Chicago, and her colleagues conducted a longitudinal study with octogenarians and found that individuals with a strong sense of purpose were significantly less susceptible to dementia. They conclude, "The tendency to derive meaning from life's experiences and to possess a sense of intentionality and goal directedness are associated with a substantially reduced risk of Alzheimer's disease and a less rapid rate of cognitive decline in older age."

CHAPTER TWO

Be a Lifelong Learner

We are all born with an intense curiosity and passion to learn. As we get older, this birthright is often obscured by the fear of failure and embarrassment. At school, most of us had little choice regarding the subjects we were supposed to learn. In art class, you had to draw. In math class, you had to do long division. In gym class, you had to play dodgeball — whether you liked it or not. Most of us have experienced the embarrassment of being pushed to perform publicly in an area in which we are unskilled. As adults, we can usually avoid the discomfort and embarrassment associated with learning something unfamiliar. We have more choice regarding what we do and what we learn. Most of us choose to focus only on those areas in which we have obvious natural talent and avoid the subjects that were sources of discomfort in the

> *Education is the best provision for old age.*
> — ARISTOTLE

past. Our negative experiences in school condition us to avoid the new, the challenging, and the unfamiliar.

Instead, break out of habitual patterns and embrace new learning with the curiosity and passion that are your birthright.

You can reclaim your birthright at any age. "No matter how old you may be at this moment, it's never too late to change your brain for the better," states neuroscientist Richard Restak, MD. "That's because the brain is different from every other organ in our body. While the liver and lungs and the kidneys wear out after a certain number of years, the brain gets sharper the more it's used. Indeed it improves with use." But what's the best way to use it?

Breaking out of your habitual patterns by embracing new learning opportunities is one of the simple secrets of revitalizing your mind. It's much easier to do this if you know that your brain is designed over millions of years of evolution to be the most profoundly powerful learning mechanism in the known universe. It also helps to understand how to make the most of your learning endeavors.

Tips for Making the Most of Your Learning

In school, most of us spent the majority of our time learning history, mathematics, social studies, and other subjects. But, unfortunately, the standard curriculum neglects the most important subject — how to learn. Here are some simple ideas that can help you enjoy learning more effectively.

- *Let go of the fear of embarrassment and failure.* The main impediment to adult learning is the fear of embarrassment and failure. Decide, as Susan Jeffers, PhD, counsels, to "feel the fear and do it anyway." Artist Georgia O'Keeffe stated, "I've been absolutely terrified every moment of my life — and I've never let it keep me from doing a single thing I wanted to do."

- *Cultivate childlike curiosity.* The best way for adults to learn is to approach new learning experiences in an open, playful way, as children do. Make learning fun. Don't take anything, especially yourself, too seriously. As Irish playwright George Bernard Shaw explained, "We don't stop playing because we grow old; we grow old because we stop playing."

> *Stimulating the brain makes it grow in every conceivable way.*
> — DR. NORMAN DOIDGE

- *Embrace the process.* The process of learning something new is more important than the result. The benefit to your brain comes from the attempt to learn. A successful outcome is a bonus.
- *Seek new challenges.* Welcome change and keep trying new things. Benjamin Franklin cautioned, "When you're finished changing, you're finished." Get out of your habit pattern. Learn something new and unfamiliar. Take a watercolor painting class, try ballroom dancing or singing lessons. Novelty yields brain benefits. Neuroscientist Michael Merzenich, PhD, and his colleagues emphasize that learning a new skill can "change hundreds of millions" of cortical connections.
- *Stretch your comfort zone.* You can accelerate your

improvement by raising the degree of difficulty of your learning challenges: for example, try more complex crossword puzzles or play chess against a more advanced opponent. Marian Diamond, PhD, the world's leading neuroanatomist, observed that rats who ran through mazes without obstruction didn't demonstrate improvements in neural complexity, but rats who were challenged by having to climb over obstacles on the way to the proverbial cheese showed significant brain growth. Dr. Diamond argues that the same principle applies to humans. She writes, "Increase the level of environmental stimulation and you will increase the branching of dendrites and the thickness of the human cortex."

- *Invest fifteen minutes every day in new learning.* Neuroscientist Daniel G. Amen, MD, points out, "Spending just 15 minutes a day learning something new is all it takes for your brain to benefit from the activity."

- *Begin it now!* Start learning something new today. You've probably noticed that as you get older, time seems to go faster. So whatever it is that you've always wanted to learn, begin it now. You'll be good at it before you know it. Neuroscientist Marco Iacoboni, MD, PhD, explains, "You can improve your mind as you age, and *now* is the best time to begin."

Lifelong Learning Is the True Fountain of Youth!

Neuroscientists agree that learning something new is one of the best ways to strengthen your brain as you age. Here are five activities that are particularly beneficial:

- Strengthening your memory
- Playing a mental sport
- Learning a new language
- Upgrading your vocabulary
- Learning to juggle

The minute a man ceases to grow, no matter what his years, that minute he begins to be old.

— WILLIAM JAMES

Below, each of these is discussed in turn.

Learn to Strengthen Your Memory: Seven Essential Memory Tips

There are seven essential tips for strengthening your memory as you age. The first one is this: Maintain a positive attitude about your memory...and...I can't recall the other six. (Just kidding!)

Memory needn't decline as you age. It's actually possible to improve it. And learning to improve your memory makes it easier to learn anything.

Memory is the mother of all wisdom.

— AESCHYLUS, Greek dramatist

In a classic psychological study entitled "The Magical Number Seven, Plus or Minus Two: Some Limits on Our Capacity for Processing Information," George A. Miller argued that the number of objects an average human can hold in working memory is seven, plus or minus two. Given that, the following are seven essential things you need to know to improve your memory throughout your life.

1. Maintain a Positive Attitude about Your Memory

If you ask any elementary school teacher what children forget in the classroom every day, you'll learn that in addition to forgetting facts, they also leave behind all sorts of things: books, pens, iPods, etc. When the teacher reminds fourth grader Jason that he left his baseball cap in the coatroom, she doesn't usually hear "What's the matter with me? I'm eight years old, and my memory is going!" or "Gosh, another junior moment!" But after age twenty-five or so, many folks begin to focus on any glitch in memory as evidence for its demise. Normal forgetting is catalogued as a "senior moment," and the decline of memory becomes a self-fulfilling prophecy. With a positive attitude, proper nutrition, exercise, and the application of the following simple tips, your memory will improve every year of your life.

2. Mobilize Your Full Attention

If you haven't registered something in your mind, then it is, of course, quite difficult to recall it. When people believe that their memory is fading, they don't bother trying to concentrate on registering new information, thus fulfilling their negative expectation. Many people complain, for example, that they can't remember names, but usually they don't focus enough to register the name in the first place. Mobilizing and focusing your attention are one of the simplest secrets to strengthening your memory.

3. Take Advantage of Your Preferred Learning Style

Visual types learn best by reading or otherwise seeing what they want to remember. Auditory learners prefer listening. They will remember the content of a book much better if they listen to it on tape or read it aloud. Individuals with a more kinesthetic learning style are more hands-on

— they learn and remember best when they are moving and physically interacting rather than sitting passively at a desk. One of the simplest ways to strengthen your recall is to learn things in your preferred mode.

4. *Connect New Information to Something You Already Know*

Recall works best by association. The more associations you create, the easier it is to remember. For example, if you want to remember someone's name, find out where he lives and what he does, then make connections in your mind with other people from the same area and/or profession.

5. *Memorize!*

Understanding isn't the same thing as remembering. It's possible to comprehend what you are reading, for example, and then forget it all immediately. Therefore, it's important to review. If you want to remember these memory tips, then reread this section later today. Take notes, and then review your notes. Then take a blank sheet of paper and, without looking at your notes or the book, re-create your notes from memory. As you attempt to do this, you strengthen the new synapses in your brain and consolidate the new learning.

Memorization is a marvelous tonic for your powers of recall. In his superb essay "In Defense of Memorization," Michael Knox Beran explains, "The memorization and recitation of the classic utterances of poets and statesmen form part of a tradition of learning that stretches back to classical antiquity, when the Greeks discovered that words and sounds — and the rhythmic patterns by which they were bound together in poetry — awakened the mind and shaped character."

You can awaken your mind and enrich your character by memorizing your favorite poems or, perhaps, the speeches or soliloquies that you find most inspiring. Begin by memorizing this wonderful poem about thinking "counterclockwise," adapted from "Youth and Age" by the Greek lyric poet Anacreon:

When I see the young men play,
Young I think I am as they,
And my aged thoughts aside,
To the dance with joy I stride;
Come, your grace and smile lend me;
Youth and mirthful thoughts attend me;
Age begone, we'll dance among
Youthful spirits, and be young;
Bring some wine and fill my glass;
Now you'll see me shake my a——;
I can dance and tipple too,
And be wild as well as you.

Over the course of twenty years of research, Helga Noice, PhD, and her husband, Tony Noice, PhD, have discovered that it's easier to remember lines, such as the lines of a poem or script, when moving in a way appropriate to the relevant character. Writing in the journal *Current Directions in Psychological Science*, the Noices explain that physical and emotional engagement facilitate recall. They received a grant from the National Institutes of Health to fund their innovative research into the benefits of theater training for older adults and have discovered that acting-based methods, including memorization, help those adults counter cognitive decline.

Here is a way to strengthen your powers of memorization, using the poem above:

- Read the poem three times.
- Read the poem three more times, aloud.
- Record your recitation, and play it back a few times before you go to sleep.
- Practice reciting two lines at a time from memory until you can do them all.
- Pretend you are a character in a Greek play. Move around and gesture as you recite the poem.

In addition to poems, you can, of course, apply the practice of memorization to anything you desire: names, story-telling, songs, jokes.

6. Teach What You Want to Remember

Teaching, or simply sharing your new learning with others, is one of the most powerful ways to consolidate learning and strengthen your memory. If you learn the samba at dance class, show your new moves to a willing friend. When you attend a reading or lecture by your favorite author, express what you learned to anyone who's available to listen.

7. Learn Memory Systems (Mnemonics) and Mind Mapping

The ancient Greeks pioneered the development of memory systems, also known as mnemonics (named after

Mnemosyne, the goddess of unlimited memory). Mnemonics were created to help orators remember the content of their speeches (notes were not allowed). In the process, the Greeks illuminated the nature of memory and discovered ways to help cultivate it throughout life.

The Greeks understood that the mind works by association — in other words, by linking one word, image, idea, or feeling with another. Recall is based on a *reliable* pattern of association, and creativity is discovering *new* patterns of association. The Greeks realized that associations can be made more reliable by applying the following principles:

- *Create images in your mind's eye.* If you wished to remember the words *dog* and *bicycle* together, you might create an image of a dog riding a bicycle.
- *Make the images specific and vivid.* What breed of dog? What color bicycle? A black Labrador on a red bicycle is easier to remember than a generic dog and bicycle.
- *Keep the elements that you are aiming to remember physically linked in your mind's eye.* Don't create an image, for example, of a dog chasing a bicycle. Why not? Because the images aren't "physically" linked in your mind's eye, and when you think of a dog you might forget what it was chasing.

Let's apply the Greek principles to memorizing something that many people have probably learned and forgotten: the planets of the solar system in order from the Sun. Take a moment and write them down or just say them aloud. (For the sake of this example, we'll include Pluto as a planet.)

Perhaps you learned a phrase to help you remember the planets, such as this one: "My Very Earnest Mother Just Served Us Nine Pizzas." The first letter of each of these words is designed to remind us of the respective planet: Mercury, Venus, Earth, Mars, Jupiter, Saturn, Uranus, Neptune, Pluto.

Although phrases can be a form of mnemonics, they don't fully employ the Greek principles and aren't as reliable as mnemonic devices that do, because you still have to remember what the letters represent. To remember the planets in order in an unforgettable way, you'll use your imaginative right hemisphere to create a vivid, visual story line as follows. (The story line does require a rudimentary knowledge of Greek/Roman mythology.)

Picture the Sun. It's hot. How hot is it? Plunge in a thermometer to find out. The thermometer boils over and out shoots a drop of *Mercury* (see it glistening in space next to the Sun). A beautiful goddess draped in gossamer robes comes floating through space to catch that drop, and she is the lovely *Venus*. She releases the drop, and it plummets into the middle of your backyard on the planet *Earth*. Your neighbor is upset by all this commotion, and he charges over to confront you. His big red face lets you know that he is the god of war, *Mars*. Then, strolling down your street, just in time to save you, comes the elegant king of the gods, *Jupiter*, clothed in regal armor. On Jupiter's breastplate, emblazoned in bright purple, are the letters S-U-N. They stand for: *Saturn*, *Uranus*, *Neptune*. And standing on Jupiter's right shoulder is a little Disney dog laughing at all this, *Pluto* (not Goofy!).

If you review this imaginative story line and create vivid

images in your mind's eye, you'll discover that it's almost impossible to forget the planets. Most people experience an immediate, dramatic improvement in their ability to remember the planets when they apply these simple memory principles. Experiencing an improvement in your ability to memorize builds confidence in your memory power. Once you realize that you can improve your memory throughout life, you'll discover a more optimistic, positive approach toward learning anything.

You can learn more about mnemonics, including how to apply them to remembering names and faces, in Tony Buzan's classic book *Master Your Memory*. Buzan also pioneered the development of another tool that will strengthen your memory (and your creative thinking ability) throughout life: Mind Maps. Most of us learned to generate, organize, and attempt to remember ideas by outlining. Outlining is a top-down, hierarchical, and unwieldy way of trying to think and remember. It overemphasizes linear, left-brain processing and doesn't involve the part of the brain that is best at memorizing — the imaginative right hemisphere.

A Mind Map is a whole-brain method for organizing and remembering things. It is structured in a way that mirrors how the brain works — in an organic, flowing, associative manner. The Mind Mapping process is easy to learn. It combines key words and images in a simple format. Studies show that Mind Mapping improves recall. Research has demonstrated that students who applied Mind Mapping scored, on average, 32 percent better on tests of recall than those who used conventional notes. The best resource for learning Mind Mapping is Tony Buzan's *The Mind Map Book*.

EXPLORE THE BRAIN FITNESS PROGRAM

Another great tool for strengthening your memory is the Brain Fitness Program developed by neuroscientist Dr. Michael Merzenich. The program utilizes visual and auditory stimuli to "speed up brain processing," "sharpen processing accuracy," and "stimulate the neuromodulatory machinery that controls recording." In a study published in the *Proceedings of the National Academy of Sciences*, Merzenich and his colleagues showed that older adults who completed the Brain Fitness Program experienced "enhancement of cognitive function." Most notably, "memory enhancement appeared to be sustained after a 3-month no-contact follow-up period."

In addition to strengthening your memory directly, you can also optimize your mental powers as the years go by, with the activities described in the rest of this chapter.

Play a Mental Sport

Novelist Raymond Chandler once remarked, "Chess is as elaborate a waste of human intelligence as you can find outside an advertising agency." It turns out, however, that Chandler was wrong about chess (although some might argue that he was probably right about advertising). Playing chess or other challenging mental sports can lower the risk of developing dementia by as much as 74 percent, according to a study conducted by researchers at the Albert Einstein College of Medicine and published in the *New England Journal of Medicine*.

The study's lead author, Joe Verghese, MD, emphasizes that the findings, collected over more than two decades, demonstrate that continuing participation in a range of mentally stimulating activities serves to protect the health of the brain. He explains, "If you exercise and build up muscles then you become more resistant to injury and other illnesses. If you exercise your brain then you are also more resistant to the effects of...illnesses such as Alzheimer's."

The researchers also discovered that, in addition to people who play chess and bridge, those who read regularly accrue significant brain benefits. Crossword puzzle enthusiasts also demonstrated a lower risk of dementia, but not as significant as that of chess and bridge players.

Although some consider playing chess and bridge to be forms of dementia in their own right, the mental gymnastics involved do exercise the brain vigorously. International grandmaster Raymond Keene is the chess columnist of the *London Times* and the world's leading expert on mental sports. According to Keene, "The infinite possibilities and rigorous complexities of the game of chess challenge the mind to ever greater levels of precision, clarity, and imagination." Keene also notes that "besides chess, the games of go and bridge offer the greatest complexity and mental challenge." Screen legend Omar Sharif, a world-class bridge player, comments, "Many games provide fun, but bridge grips you. It exercises your mind. Your mind can rust, you know, but bridge prevents the rust from forming." Learn chess or bridge to stimulate your brain's infinite possibilities and prevent cognitive rust.

TUNE YOUR BRAIN AND YOUR HORMONES —
LEARN A MUSICAL INSTRUMENT

The Music Making and Wellness Project, an international collaboration between experts in music therapy, medicine, biochemistry, psychology, psychiatry, gerontology, and keyboard pedagogy, found that older adults who took music lessons showed measurable improvements in their sense of well-being (including lower levels of anxiety, depression, and loneliness) compared with a control group. And their blood tests indicated a 90 percent increase in levels of human growth hormone, the hormone associated with youthful energy and sexual function.

A contributor to the study, Professor Midori Koga, explains her inspiration: "My grandfather began taking violin lessons in his late 70s....he seemed to fall in love with music. In Japan, the 88th birthday of a man's life is considered an important milestone. As my grandfather approached this event, he decided that he would like to present his first concert to celebrate the special day. The concert was a lovely, memorable experience for all involved, and there wasn't a dry eye in the hall. Those of us who loved him dearly were touched at the way he responded to his music; he played as a child plays, with joy, heart and pure abandon....He used to say, 'This is keeping me young! I wake up each morning happy to know that I have so much to learn today.' "

Learn to Speak a New Language

Learning to speak a new language is one of the most effective ways to keep your mind sharp as you prevent memory loss and other symptoms associated with age-related ailments. And, as with the other activities that strengthen your mind over the years, you don't have to become an expert to get the benefits. "You don't have to master it," explains Andrew Weil, MD, author of *Healthy Aging*. "Just the attempt to learn a language is like running different software through the brain."

Leonardo da Vinci taught himself Latin when he was forty years old so that he could read the classics that were becoming available due to the invention of the printing press. Now, thanks to a range of excellent accelerated-learning immersion courses and brain-friendly software programs, language learning for adults is much easier than it was in Leonardo's day.

Despite these remarkable advances in language-learning strategy and technology, many adults still believe, erroneously, that learning a new language is much easier for children and almost impossible in middle age and beyond. However, a growing body of research demonstrates that older people *can* learn new languages, and that *adults may actually be better and faster language learners than children.*

When I was young I was amazed at Plutarch's statement that the elder Cato began at the age of eighty to learn Greek. I am amazed no longer. Old age is ready to undertake tasks that youth shirked because they would take too long.

— W. SOMERSET MAUGHAM

"Studies comparing the rate of second language acquisition in children and adults have shown that...in the long run, adults actually learn languages more quickly than children," reports Mary J. Schleppegrell, PhD, of the University of Michigan. She adds, "Learning ability does not decline with age. If older people remain healthy, their intellectual abilities and skills do not decline."

Traditional academic language programs were based on an overly analytical "left-brained" approach. Classes focused on verb conjugations and vocabulary words. It didn't work very well. The secret of effective adult language learning is to re-create the original learning approach of childhood, involving students in experiences that emphasize context and action more than theory and abstractions.

For example, in a progressive French class, students don berets and wield baguettes. The walls are plastered with colorful posters of Paris and the French countryside. An Édith Piaf recording graces the proceedings. The students are acting out a scene using only French. When a mistake is made, the teacher simply models the correct word, usage, or pronunciation, which the student then repeats. The teacher aims to "catch the students doing something right." Emphasis is placed on expressive gesture and body language. The room is filled with animation, laughter, and joie de vivre. This playful approach to learning isn't just more fun; it's much faster and more effective.

The remarkably successful Rosetta Stone language-learning software, used by NASA and Thomson Reuters, among many other institutions, is based on this more natural, intuitive approach to learning. As their website explains, "We've eliminated the traditional approach of using translation and grammar rules, empowering you to think in your new language. There are no flash cards, dictionaries or memorization drills.... By surrounding you with words, images and the voices of native speakers... you progress naturally from words and phrases to sentences and conversations."

Learn a new language and get a new soul.

— Czech proverb

Learning a new language opens up new worlds of thought, imagination, and connection. The great filmmaker Federico Fellini commented, "A different language is a different vision of life." This expanded vision of life strengthens your memory and your resistance to age-related cognitive difficulties. A study published in the journal *Psychology and Aging* reported that subjects who spoke a second language "responded more rapidly to conditions that placed greater demands on working memory." The researchers noted that the benefits of bilingualism were "greater for older participants" and concluded that "there is a correlation between bilingualism and the offset of age-related cognitive losses."

Upgrade Your Vocabulary

In addition to learning a new language, it's also helpful to continually upgrade your vocabulary in your primary language. Leonardo da Vinci's notebooks contain hundreds of words that he copied, along with definitions, to strengthen his facility for words in his native Italian. As Leonardo understood, the best way to improve your vocabulary is to write down words you want to learn and then practice using them in context. You can find new words to learn by reading avidly, enjoying Scrabble or crossword puzzles, and exploring the dictionary. For example, you can subscribe to an online word-of-the-day service such as the excellent one offered by Merriam-Webster (www.merriam-webster.com/word-of-the-day/). You can also find iPhone apps for chess, bridge, Scrabble, Sudoku, and many other "brain games."

Many studies show that a strong vocabulary correlates with success in life. Psychometrician Johnson O'Connor conducted pioneering research demonstrating that vocabulary level was the single strongest predictor of occupational success in a wide range of disciplines. Moreover, O'Connor emphasized that because vocabulary can be strengthened throughout life, it was a simple and profound secret for cultivating human potential and improving the mind with age.

Juggle Your Way to a Younger Brain

In a January 2004 news bulletin, the BBC led with the headline "Juggling 'Can Boost Brain Power.'" The same day, CNN reported, "Juggling Good for the Brain, Study Shows." A few days later, a headline in *Medical News Today* read, "Juggling Makes Your Brain Bigger — New Study."

What was the inspiration for these global headlines? The publication in the January 22, 2004, edition of the scientific journal *Nature* of an article entitled "Neuroplasticity: Changes in Grey Matter Induced by Training." The article, published by a team of

Iron rusts from disuse; stagnant water loses its purity… even so does inaction sap the vigor of the mind.

— LEONARDO DA VINCI

HOW TO JUGGLE

Find three balls and get started now by following these simple instructions.

1. Stand in a balanced, upright posture and enjoy a few deep, full breaths, allowing generous exhalations. Start with one ball and toss it back and forth, from hand to hand, in a gentle arc just above your head.
2. Take two balls, one in each hand. Toss the ball in your right hand; when it reaches its high point, toss the ball in your left hand in the same manner. Focus on smooth, easy throws, and *let both balls drop*.
3. Same as step 2, only this time, catch the first toss. Let the second one drop.
4. Same as step 2, only this time, catch both tosses.
5. Now you are ready to try three balls (you'll be truly juggling now because you'll have more balls than hands). Take two balls in one hand and one in the other. Toss the front ball in the hand that has two balls. When it reaches its high point, throw the single ball in your other hand. When that reaches its high point, throw the remaining ball. Do not try to catch them; just relax, and *let them all drop*.
6. Same as step 5, only this time, catch the first toss.
7. Same as step 5, only this time, catch the first two tosses. If you catch the first two balls and remember to throw the third, you will notice that there is only one ball remaining in the air. Catch the third ball. Guess what? You're juggling!

German researchers, described the effects of regular juggling practice on the adult brain. The researchers found that fifteen minutes of daily juggling practice over the course of three months resulted in a significant increase in the brain's gray matter. The nonjuggling control group showed no improvements in the brain.

The study was a landmark in our understanding of the brain's ability to effectively re-create itself over time with appropriate training. The researchers also found, however, that the brain benefits began to fade after the subjects stopped regular juggling practice. The research team summarized its findings by stating simply, "The brain is like a muscle, we need to exercise it."

Another study, published in 2006 by German researchers, compared progress in three-ball juggling performance between people from different age groups. After simple instructions were given, all subjects, ranging in age from fifteen to eighty-nine, engaged in a series of six practice sessions. The over-sixty group learned quickly and effectively. The researchers concluded, "Older adults exhibit high reserve capacity, that is, a potential for learning new motor skills."

Learning memory systems, mental sports, new languages, new vocabulary, and juggling are all wonderful ways to maintain a vibrant, lively mind. Other especially beneficial activities include dance, creative writing, tai chi, cooking, drawing, and becoming computer and web savvy. Although these activities offer special benefits, the greatest benefit probably accrues from your engagement with *any* activity that is new and challenging. As neuroscientist Daniel G. Amen, MD, emphasizes, "New learning actually causes new connections to form in your brain.... It has a positive effect on your brain and can help keep it young. The best mental exercise is acquiring new knowledge and doing things you haven't done before."

If I had to live my life again I would have made a rule to read some poetry and listen to some music at least once a week; for perhaps the parts of my brain now atrophied could thus have been kept active through use.

— CHARLES DARWIN

Lifelong Learning, Wisdom, and Happiness

What's the single greatest factor contributing to happiness and fulfillment as we age? Wisdom! More than two millennia ago, the Greek playwright Sophocles observed, "Wisdom is the supreme part of happiness." Contemporary research supports the ancient playwright's musing. A study coauthored by Paul B. Baltes, PhD, former director of the Center of Lifespan Psychology at the Max Planck Institute for Human Development in Berlin, explains, "Lifelong learning and continued education are essential for older people who want to stay involved in a rapidly changing world. However, in the later years of life, it may be even more important to acquire the timeless and universal knowledge of wisdom." Gerontologist Monika Ardelt,

PhD, concurs. She summarizes the results of her extensive investigations by stating, "Wisdom has a profoundly positive influence on life satisfaction independent of objective circumstances."

What is wisdom? Dr. Baltes's study defines it as "an expert knowledge system concerning the fundamental pragmatics of life." It has a lot to do with perspective, and it's manifest in gratitude, forgiveness, and humor. William James quipped that it is "the art of knowing what to overlook." Wisdom includes accurately assessing and serenely accepting the things we can't change, and finding the courage to continue pursuing our goals in alignment with our deepest purpose, especially when faced with adversity. Recent studies also suggest a correlation between our tenure on the planet and the depth of our wisdom.

Marc E. Agronin, MD, a geriatric psychiatrist and author of *How We Age*, treats patients in their eighties, nineties, and beyond. Although many of his patients are confronted with the maladies and infirmities associated with getting older, Dr. Agronin believes that "the problems of aging must be weighed against the promises." As he sees it, "aging equals vitality, wisdom, creativity, spirit and ultimately hope."

CHAPTER THREE

Exercise for More Brain Power

Walter M. Bortz, MD, is coauthor of *The Roadmap to 100: The Breakthrough Science of Living a Long and Healthy Life*. You might imagine that "breakthrough science" refers to some form of stem-cell therapy, genetic-modification serum, hormone cocktail, or perhaps the latest supersupplement. But Bortz, who is also author of *Living Longer for Dummies*, reveals that the real secret to a long and healthy life is *regular exercise and a healthy diet*.

Dr. Bortz offers peer-validated research to support his contention that fitness is the most important component of healthy aging. A veteran of more than forty marathons, Bortz is, at age eighty, a great exemplar of his own approach. He explains, "Almost everything we have been taught about growing older has been wrong. Frailty, heart disease, loss of an active sex life, and memory loss, are just a few problems typically associated with aging. All of these symptoms have less to do with chronology than with lack of conditioning. You can have a long, *healthy* life. The good news is that you can gain vitality even in advanced ages. My research has proven this over and over again." Bortz concludes, "Exercise provides a 30-year age offset." In other words, conditioning trumps chronology.

The notion that physical fitness is crucial to overall health and mental acuity was a cornerstone of the philosophy of ancient Greece and Rome. Plato observed, "Lack of activity destroys the good condition of every human being, while movement and methodical physical exercise save it and preserve it." And Hippocrates advised, "If we could give every individual the right amount of nourishment and exercise, not too little and not too much, we would have found the safest way to health. For this is the great error of our day that the physicians separate the soul from the body."

> *All parts of the body which have a function, if used in moderation and exercised in labors in which each is accustomed, become thereby healthy, well developed and age more slowly, but if unused they become liable to disease, defective in growth and age quickly.*
>
> — HIPPOCRATES

The Latin phrase *Mens sana in corpore sano* — "a healthy mind in a healthy body" — was one of the mottoes that inspired Leonardo da Vinci. About a hundred years after the death of Leonardo, philosopher René Descartes codified the distinction between mind and body in his book *Meditations on First Philosophy: In Which the Existence of God and the Distinction of the Soul from the Body Are Demonstrated*. This seminal work contributed to the modern tendency for educators and physicians to view these aspects of the self as disconnected.

Contemporary science demonstrates that Descartes was wrong and Hippocrates was right: mind and body are inseparable. Attitude influences physical well-being and longevity, and physical exercise influences the brain and our mental acuity.

In his superb book *Brain Rules*, molecular biologist John Medina, PhD, introduces his first rule for improving your mind as you get older: exercise boosts brain power! Medina explains that a "Brain Rule" is based on something that science knows with certainty. He writes, "Exercise zaps harmful stress chemicals. It boosts problem-solving, planning and attention." Furthermore, he adds, "*It cuts risk of dementia in half.*"

THE REVOLUTIONARY NEW SCIENCE OF EXERCISE AND THE BRAIN

In *Spark: The Revolutionary New Science of Exercise and the Brain*, John J. Ratey, MD, professor of psychiatry at Harvard Medical School, explains that in addition to promoting better muscle tone and cardiovascular fitness, exercise is "one of the best treatments we have for most psychiatric problems." Ratey presents compelling research demonstrating the efficacy of exercise in sharpening cognition and memory, and in overcoming anxiety, stress, and depression.

Why is exercise so effective in helping to improve your mind as you age? The main reason is that it is one of the best ways to ensure that your brain is getting enough fresh air. Your brain is about 2 percent of your body weight but uses more than 20 percent of your oxygen intake. Years of sedentary behavior and poor dietary habits can result in sluggish arterial blood flow to the brain, causing interference with memory and other mental functions. John J. Ratey, MD, explains that exercise "unleashes a cascade of neurochemicals and growth factors" that serve to counter the effects of age. He adds, "The neurons in the brain connect to one another through 'leaves' on treelike branches, and exercise causes those branches to grow and bloom with new buds, thus enhancing brain function at a fundamental level."

In a fascinating experiment, people in their seventies were given a series of short-term memory tests, after which they spent fifteen minutes in an oxygen tent. When they were retested after the oxygen exposure, their scores improved significantly. Researchers discovered similar improvements following surgery to clear the carotid arteries (the primary conduits of blood and oxygen to the brain). Keep your brain oxygenated and your mind sharp by maintaining a fitness regimen that includes cardiovascular, strength, flexibility, and balance training. Before giving you an overview of these four complementary areas of exercise, we'll consider some of the keys to getting the most out of any fitness program.

Keys to Getting the Most out of a Fitness Program

Here are some of the most effective ways to get the greatest benefit out of an exercise program.

- *Find activities you enjoy.* One of the secrets of fitness is to find activities that you want to do, which increases your motivation for doing them. Some people like to go to the gym and hoist iron, while others prefer dancing, biking, or yoga. Experiment with different fitness activities to find the ones that are most fun for you.
- *Overcome inertia.* If you are out of shape, you may feel that the only activity you enjoy is resting on the couch. Nevertheless, you will discover that if you get up and exercise, you will always be glad you did. Imagine the feeling of relaxation and exhilaration that comes from a good workout, and let that feeling magnetize you up off the couch and into activity.
- *Begin gently, and gradually increase the level of challenge.* When you do aerobic exercise or lift weights appropriately, your cells send messages to your brain that say, "Please expand the blood supply." The results are greater cardiovascular capacity and stronger muscles. But if you overdo it, your cells will send a message that says, "We don't want to do this anymore!" It's also a good idea to gently warm up in preparation for exercise and then give yourself enough time to cool down when you finish. An appropriate warm-up increases the flow of synovial fluid in your joints and blood to your muscles in a way that helps lower the risk of injury. It also helps prepare you psychologically for optimal performance. The primary aim of the cooldown is to promote

recovery from the demands you've placed on your system through exercising.

- *Quit while you're ahead.* A corollary of the previous principle, this is an important piece of common sense that is often forgotten. If you stop exercising while you are still enjoying it, then you create a positive "recency effect" (the term psychologists use to describe the tendency to remember the last thing in a series). The positive feeling at the end of your exercise period makes it much easier to look forward to your next session.

- *Form is almost everything.* The way you do an exercise is profoundly important. If your body is contorted to do a stretch or lift a weight, you will do more harm than good.

- *Make exercise part of your everyday life.* It's great to go to the gym or to a dance class, because specialized activities such as these are efficient ways to concentrate the benefits of exercise. But you will get much better results over the long term if you also embrace fitness opportunities in everyday life. For example, whenever you can, take the stairs instead of the elevator, walk around your desk when you are speaking on the phone, walk or cycle to nearby destinations, and stretch when you are in line at the airport or supermarket.

- *No brain, no gain.* Let go of the outdated and destructive notion of "no pain, no gain." Instead, use your intelligence to make the most of every workout.

Bring mindful attention to your exercise to lower the risk of injury and enhance the joy of movement.

Complementary Areas of Fitness

An ideal fitness program incorporates complementary areas of fitness, including cardiovascular conditioning, strength and flexibility training, and the cultivation of balance and poise. These dimensions of fitness all serve to support the vigor of your body and the cheerfulness of your soul.

Exercise ferments the humors, casts them into their proper channels, throws off redundancies, and helps nature in those secret distributions, without which the body cannot subsist in its vigor, nor the soul act with cheerfulness.

— JOSEPH ADDISON, British author

Aerobic Conditioning: Oxygenate Your Brain

Aerobics was published in 1968 by Kenneth H. Cooper, MD, of the U.S. Air Force School of Aerospace Medicine. Cooper established scientifically what Plato and Hippocrates had counseled more than two thousand years before: regular exercise is essential for the health of mind and body. Cooper emphasizes the strong relationship between physical fitness, mental acuity, and emotional well-being.

Also known as "cardio," aerobic exercise focuses on strengthening your endurance by increasing your heart rate. Aerobic exercise inspires deeper and faster breathing, thereby raising the level of oxygen in your bloodstream. As you develop aerobic fitness, your heart, lungs, and blood vessels become more efficient at delivering oxygen to all the cells of your body, including your brain cells. And, since your brain uses more than 20 percent of your body's oxygen, aerobic fitness is especially important in maintaining brain health as we age.

Thirty minutes of aerobic activity three times a week improves scores on memory tests and may reverse the effects of aging, according to a study coauthored by James A. Blumenthal, PhD, of the Duke University Medical Center. Duke University research has found that "aerobic exercise may not only lift depression in the middle-aged and elderly, but also improve memory, planning, organization, and the ability to juggle several mental tasks at the same time." As Dr. Blumenthal notes, regular aerobic exercise may be able to "offset some of the mental declines often associated with the aging process." You can get aerobic benefits from all kinds of activities — shoveling snow, raking leaves, gardening, chopping wood, even operating your vacuum cleaner. But the activities that represent some of the most efficient and effective means for aerobic development are walking, running, cycling, dancing, and swimming.

Walking

Brisk walking is one of the simplest and most natural forms of exercise. It is low impact and doesn't require any special equipment; and you don't need a class to learn how to do it. In addition to cardiovascular benefits, walking helps to regulate metabolism and hormone production in a way that makes it easier to maintain healthy body weight. Walking also sharpens memory, according to a study in the *European Journal of Developmental Psychology* entitled "Cognitive performance is improved while walking." And walking is a time-honored way to boost creative problem-solving ability.

> *Walking is the best possible exercise.*
> — THOMAS JEFFERSON

The ancient Latin phrase "Solvitas perambulatorum" translates as "solve it by walking."

Running

In a classic study, Fred H. Gage, PhD, and his colleagues compared mice that ran freely in mazes with those that did the rodent equivalent of sitting on the couch, drinking beer, and watching television. After about three months, the running rats had developed twice as many new brain cells and demonstrated superior performance in maze-solving ability. The researchers concluded that physical activity regulates "neurogenesis, synaptic plasticity, and learning."

You needn't run on a wheel to get the benefits for your body and brain, but to preserve your joints, it is best to run on grass or dirt — or on a treadmill or elliptical machine — rather than on concrete or asphalt.

Cycling

Riding a bicycle, either stationary or mobile, is another great way to get (and stay) in shape. Spinning classes use different levels of resistance on stationary bikes to create an intense, concentrated workout. Many people find that the inspirational music played in spinning classes makes it easier to keep pedaling.

Dancing

Dancing is an effective all-around workout. The German author Johann Paul Friedrich Richter (also known as Jean Paul) explained, "Other exercises develop single powers and muscles, but dancing embellishes, exercises, and equalizes all the muscles at once." And the Austrian author and musician Vicki Baum noted, "There are short-cuts to happiness, and dancing is one of them."

Swimming

The buoyancy of water makes swimming one of the safest forms of low-impact exercise. Additionally, water offers twelve times more resistance than air, so moving through the pool is an efficient way to condition your cardiovascular and musculoskeletal systems.

A study led by Steven N. Blair, PhD, of the University of South Carolina found that swimmers had higher cardiovascular fitness levels than walkers and sedentary people. Swimmers live longer as well: in a study of more than forty thousand men between twenty and ninety years of age, swimmers were 50 percent more likely to be alive at the end of the thirty-two-year study period than walkers, runners, or those with a sedentary lifestyle. As Blair pointed out, "This is the first report that examined mortality rates among swimmers in comparison with other types of physical activity and sedentary lifestyle. We conclude that men who swim for exercise have better survival rates than their sedentary peers."

FOR BEST RESULTS, PICK UP THE PACE

Research demonstrates that shorter, high-intensity workouts may yield better results than traditional endurance training. Izumi Tabata, PhD, of the National Institute of Health and Nutrition in Tokyo and his colleagues studied two groups of cyclists. One group did long-duration, medium-intensity training sessions, while the other practiced brief, high-intensity routines. After six weeks, the high-intensity group showed much greater improvement in key measures of fitness such as lung capacity and oxygen utilization.

Al Sears, MD, originator of the Progressive Accelerated Cardiovascular Exertion (PACE) program, explains that shorter, high-intensity training sessions, featuring an appropriate balance of activity and recovery, produce powerful benefits, including the following:

- Quicker cardiac adjustments to changes in demand, which is a key factor in lowering the risk of heart attacks
- More efficient burning of excess body fat
- Improved cholesterol levels — a decrease in total cholesterol and an increase in "good" cholesterol
- Raised testosterone levels, which helps to prevent memory loss, accumulation of fat, low libido, sexual dysfunction, and loss of strength and bone

The best aspect of the PACE system is that, compared with traditional endurance training regimens, you can achieve superior results in much less time.

Strength Training: Less Fat, Stronger Bones

Strength training is another essential component of your fitness program. Just three twenty-minute sessions per week can yield profound benefits. Strength training develops bone density and resilience as it builds and tones your muscles. Increased muscle mass helps you regulate your percentage of body fat and maintain a more youthful metabolism.

The benefits of strength training are available throughout life. In a study reported in the *New England Journal of Medicine*, researchers from Tufts University engaged nursing home residents in a ten-week program of supervised weight training. The researchers concluded, "A high-intensity, progressive regimen of resistance training improves muscle strength and size in frail elderly people." Other studies confirm that weight training with either free weights or machines helps to restore diminished bone density, reduce arthritic pains, and dramatically increase functional strength.

If you're starting a strength-training program for the first time, it's a good idea to take a class or engage a trainer if you can afford it. Proper form and the right blend of exercises are very important, to avoid injury and maximize the benefits. Resistance machines are helpful for beginners because they encourage good form. Free weights and resistance bands can also be very effective. If you want to understand the practical anatomy of strength training, read Frédéric Delavier's *Strength Training Anatomy*.

Flexibility: Increase Your Life Extension

The word *flexibility* derives from the Latin *flectere* (to bend). Flexibility is our capacity to bend without doing

FUNCTIONAL STRENGTH

Functional strength is the type of strength we need in everyday life: for carting a few bags of groceries, placing your carry-on bag in the overhead compartment, or ascending a steep stairway. Functional strength is a key element in maintaining mobility and freedom of movement as you age. The best way to cultivate this very practical approach to fitness is to practice classical calisthenics.

Calisthenics is derived from the Greek *kalos* (beautiful) and *sthenos* (strength), and the practice of calisthenics focuses on moving your own body weight. As Dr. Al Sears explains, "Nature designed your body to build and maintain muscle in response to the demands of your own body weight." Sears adds that "calisthenics are the most effective way to improve bone density, metabolism and immune function."

Part of the beauty of developing your strength through calisthenics is that you can do them anywhere, anytime without expensive equipment: squats, push-ups, sit-ups, dips, and pull-ups are simple and very effective. (And they still serve as the core strength-training regimen for those whose lives depend on functional strength: U.S. Green Berets and Navy SEALs!)

ourselves harm. The McGraw-Hill *Concise Dictionary of Modern Medicine* defines it this way: "The ability of a muscle or extremity to relax and yield to stretch and stress forces; the ROM (range of motion) of a joint." This definition suggests that flexibility is more about releasing and relaxing than forcing a muscle or system of muscles to elongate.

We are designed to move, but if we spend years sitting at a desk, we begin to compromise our freedom of movement. Stiffness and rigidity are not symptoms of aging per se but, rather, the consequence of years of sedentary living. Like cardiovascular fitness and strength, flexibility can be cultivated at any age, and flexibility training will complement your aerobic and strength development endeavors. Here are some guidelines.

- Remember that flexibility is a function of releasing and relaxing rather than forcing change. "Stretching" is de-contracting.
- Warm up before you practice flexibility exercises. A few minutes on an exercise bike or elliptical machine will help you prevent injury and stretch more effectively.
- Avoid bouncing. Never force the extension of your range of movement. Flexibility exercises shouldn't be painful.
- Take your time and breathe. Give yourself at least thirty seconds for each de-contraction. Breathe fully and deeply as you allow muscles to release.
- Make flexibility awareness part of your everyday life. Be mindful when you stretch to reach something on a high shelf, and relax and exhale as you turn your head to see what's behind you before pulling out of a parking space.
- Study yoga. Over the course of thousands of years, yoga adepts have discovered extraordinarily effective means to cultivate flexibility of body and mind.

Dean Ornish, MD, founder of the Preventive Medicine Research Institute in Sausalito, California, prescribes yoga as a powerful method for reversing the effects of age-related ailments. It's best to learn yoga from an experienced teacher. And if you can't find a class nearby, then read *The Pocket Idiot's Guide to 108 Yoga Poses* by Ami Jayaprada Hirschstein.

- Learn the physiology of flexibility. *Stretching Anatomy*, coauthored by Arnold G. Nelson, PhD, associate professor in the Department of Kinesiology at Louisiana State University, is a great resource for understanding the how and why of flexibility. We also recommend *Framework* by Nicholas A. DiNubile, an orthopedic surgeon at the University of Pennsylvania Hospital in Philadelphia. Dr. DiNubile offers a comprehensive, practical program of rehabilitative exercises to improve overall fitness and flexibility.

Balance and Poise: The Missing Links in Healthy Aging

Balance and poise are often the critical missing links in fitness programs. Since loss of balance and poise increase the risk of injury from falls, this aspect of fitness becomes more important as we get older.

Balance is physical equilibrium. It's also defined as harmony between apparently contrasting elements and an aesthetically pleasing integration of opposing elements. Poise is grace in action. It's an expression of the optimal distribution of energy — the right amount, in the right place, at the right time. It correlates significantly with social grace and composure.

Our physical balance and poise have a profound effect on our dignity, composure, and grace throughout life. We can also prevent the age-related frailty associated with loss of balance and poise with some simple practices, such as

- Single-leg standing
- Curb walking
- Use of balance-training devices
- The Alexander technique
- Tai chi

Let's look at each of these in turn.

Single-Leg Standing

Standing on one leg, like a flamingo, is one of the simplest ways to cultivate balance. Practice balancing on one leg and then the other. Pick a point straight ahead of you and focus your eyes on that point as you balance. (It's best to stand near something stable, like a table or wall, so you can use your hands to steady yourself if necessary.) After you can balance on each leg for about thirty seconds, try the exercise with your eyes closed. At first, you may be surprised at how difficult it is to maintain your balance with closed eyes, but keep practicing. The current world record for standing on one leg with closed eyes (while holding an umbrella!) is two minutes.

Curb Walking

Practice walking on a curb or balancing on a two-by-four. It may sound strange, but you will be in good company:

"People in the cars think I'm crazy, but it doesn't bother me," explains Marian C. Diamond, the world's leading neuroanatomist. Diamond practices curb walking most mornings on her way to work at the University of California. She says, "I know it's good for the cerebellum…it's just like a balance beam." She refers to curb walking as a simple way to "sharpen the brain's control center for physical coordination."

Use of Balance-Training Devices

Balance boards (also known as wobble or rocker boards), core balance discs (round, partially inflated cushions), and BOSU balls (half a large ball set on a frame) are designed for balance training. You can learn how to use all of these tools in *The Great Balance and Stability Handbook* by Andre Noel Potvin and Chad Benson.

The Alexander Technique: The Performer's Trade Secret for Balance and Poise

The Alexander technique is a simple, effective method for cultivating balance and poise throughout life. A trade secret among professional performers, including luminaries such as Paul Newman, Mary Steenburgen, Sting, Helena Bonham Carter, Paul McCartney, Sir Georg Solti, and John Cleese, the technique is part of the curriculum at the Royal Academy of Dramatic Arts, the Juilliard School, and other top academies for musicians, actors, and dancers.

The best way to learn the Alexander technique is private instruction with a qualified teacher. Alexander technique teachers are trained to use their hands in an extraordinarily subtle and delicate way to guide you to rediscover your natural alignment, poise, and balance. You can also try the following simple exercise, the balanced resting state, prescribed by Alexander technique teachers to promote better balance and poise.

THE BALANCED RESTING STATE:
LENGTHEN YOUR SPINE TO REALIGN

All you need to benefit from this procedure is a relatively quiet place, some carpeted floor space, a few paperback books, and fifteen to twenty minutes.

Begin by placing the books on the floor. Stand approximately your body's length away from the books with your feet a shoulder width apart. Let your hands rest gently at your sides. Facing away from the books, look straight ahead with a soft, alert focus. Pause for a few moments.

Think of allowing your neck to be free so that your head can go forward and up, and your whole torso can lengthen and widen. Breathing freely, become aware of the contact of your feet with the floor and notice the distance from your feet to the top of your head. Keep your eyes open and alive, and listen to the sounds around you.

Moving lightly and easily, sit on the floor. Supporting yourself with your hands, which should be placed behind you, put your feet on the floor in front of you, with your knees bent. Continue breathing easily.

Let your head drop forward a bit to ensure that you are not tightening your neck muscles and pulling your head back. Then gently roll your spine along the floor so that your head rests on the books. The books should be positioned so that they support your head at the place where your neck ends and your head begins. If your head is not well positioned, reach back with one hand and support your head while using the other hand to place the books in the proper position. Add or take books away until you find a height that encourages a gentle lengthening of your neck muscles. Your feet should remain flat on the floor, with your knees pointing up to the ceiling and your hands resting on the floor or loosely folded on your chest. Allow the weight of your body to be fully supported by the floor.

Rest in this position for fifteen to twenty minutes. As you rest, gravity will lengthen your spine and realign your torso. Keep your eyes open to avoid dozing off. Bring your attention to the flow of your breathing and to the gentle pulsation of your whole body. Be aware of the ground supporting your back, allowing your shoulders to rest as your back widens. Let your neck be free as your whole body lengthens and expands.

After you have rested for fifteen to twenty minutes, get up slowly, being careful to avoid stiffening or shortening your body as you return to a standing position. In order to achieve a smooth transition, decide when you are going to move and then gently roll over onto your front, maintaining your new sense of integration and expansion. Ease your way into a crawling position, and then up onto one knee. With your head leading the movement upward, stand up.

Pause for a few moments. Listen. Again feel your feet on the floor and notice the distance between your feet and the top of your head. You may be surprised to discover that the distance has expanded. As you move into the activities of your day, think about not doing anything that interferes with this expansion, ease, and overall uplift (such as hunching over your steering wheel while driving, clasping your toothbrush with a death grip, or raising your shoulders to slice a carrot in the kitchen).

For best results, practice the balanced resting state twice a day. You can do it when you wake up in the morning, when you come home from work, or before retiring at night. The procedure is especially valuable when you feel overworked or stressed. Regular practice will help you develop an upright, easy poise in everything you do.

THE ALEXANDER TECHNIQUE OFFERS LONG-TERM BENEFITS

The Alexander technique proved to be an effective and enduring means for overcoming chronic back pain, according to a study reported in the *British Medical Journal*. Although previous research had demonstrated short-term benefits of Alexander technique lessons, this was the first attempt to measure the benefits over an extended time period. Researchers compared the effectiveness of counseling, massage, exercise programs, and a series of lessons in the Alexander technique with more than five hundred patients. The objective of the comprehensive and carefully controlled study was to determine the effectiveness of lessons in the Alexander technique.

The conclusion? "One to one lessons in the Alexander technique from registered teachers have long term benefits for patients with chronic back pain."

Tai Chi: The Way of Invigoration

Originally developed as a powerful martial art, tai chi is a Chinese system of movement that hones balance and poise. It is practiced by millions of Chinese as an integral approach to healthy aging, and in the past thirty years, it has become more available in the West. Peter M. Wayne, PhD, of the Harvard Medical School confirms its importance by noting, "A growing body of carefully conducted research is building a compelling case for tai chi as an adjunct to standard medical treament for the prevention and rehabilitation of many conditions commonly associated with age."

Tai Chi Chuan, the great ultimate, strengthens the weak, raises the sick, invigorates the debilitated, and encourages the timid.... Soft sinews are a special characteristic of the infant. If people who are not far from death are to have any hope of returning to youthfulness, it is only through concentrating on the chi and becoming soft.

— PROFESSOR CHENG MAN-CH'ING, tai chi grandmaster

Although there are a number of different styles of tai chi, they are all characterized by fluid, slow, and graceful movements. This "meditation in motion" has surprising benefits. According to another researcher from Harvard Medical School, Gloria Yeh, MD, "Tai chi strengthens both the lower and upper extremities and also the core muscles of the back and abdomen." Furthermore, Steven L. Wolf, PhD, and his colleagues at the Emory University School of Medicine found that older adults who participated in a fifteen-week tai chi program reported significant improvements in balance, and they reduced their risk of falling by almost 50 percent.

It's best to learn tai chi from an accomplished teacher, but once you learn a form, you can practice it on your own.

Maybe you prefer tai chi, yoga, or Pilates. Or perhaps you just like to walk, run, or swim. In any case, some form of daily movement practice is essential to your well-being, and it becomes even more important as you get older. Whatever your stage in life or your current state of conditioning, you can become fitter, stronger, and more flexible, balanced, and poised, starting today. A regular program of intelligent exercise will raise your core vitality, elevate your daily baseline of happiness, help prevent injury and illness, and — by oxygenating your brain — play a key role in improving your mind as you age.

CHAPTER FOUR

Mind Your Diet to Nourish Your Mind

Five hundred years ago, Leonardo da Vinci gave advice on healthy eating that is timeless and essential. The maestro counseled eating fresh, wholesome, natural foods. He emphasized the importance of dining in a relaxed and enjoyable setting, and advised that we enjoy a little red wine with dinner. He also advocated being present and appreciative of the *experience* of dining, an example of what we now call mindfulness.

The doctor of the future will no longer treat the human frame with drugs, but rather will cure and prevent disease with nutrition.

— THOMAS EDISON

Leonardo is renowned as perhaps the greatest genius of all time, but you don't have to be a genius to recognize that his advice was based on what we refer to today as a Mediterranean diet. Diet fads come and go, but there are some universal, timeless truths about healthy eating that will be summarized in this chapter. And, as Leonardo understood, healthy eating can help to optimize your brain functioning in a pleasurable way.

Scientists estimate that the average human body is composed of fifty to seventy-five trillion cells. And all of those cells, including your one hundred billion neurons, are completely reconstructed more than twice a year. Your diet provides the fuel for this cellular renewal. As Daniel G. Amen, MD, emphasizes, "If you want to have a great brain, you must consistently give it nutrient-rich foods. This is one of the easiest, most effective strategies to boost brain power quickly."

Although some jest that the secret of longevity is to give up everything that makes you want to live longer, you needn't actually experience deprivation to be healthy. Healthy eating is *more* pleasurable. There are seven essential elements for an enjoyable, healthy diet. These include the following:

1. Maintaining hydration
2. Starting your day with breakfast
3. Rustproofing your brain and body
4. Minimizing or eliminating the unnecessary
5. Supplementing for a sharper mind
6. Embracing moderation
7. Enjoying dining

In this chapter, we will explore each of these seven elements.

I. Maintaining Hydration

Just as you must water your garden regularly to maintain the health of your plants, you must also provide plenty of water for the blossoming of your brain and the health of your body. Water is a critical and often overlooked factor in nutrition. Your brain is 80 percent water, and water is an essential contributor to all of the body's metabolic processes. The amount of water you need every day depends on a range of factors, including your activity level, weight, the relative humidity in your environment, and your general health; but the average prescription is eight to ten eight-ounce glasses of pure water daily. You can complement your water intake by enjoying plenty of fresh fruits and vegetables with high water content.

> *Water is the driving force of all nature.*
>
> — LEONARDO DA VINCI

Dehydration is a common cause, or exacerbating factor, of a range of ailments, from headaches to joint pain. Dehydration also raises cortisol and other stress hormone levels, thereby interfering with clarity of thought and memory acuity. It's a sneaky condition — most folks aren't aware that they are suffering from some degree of dehydration. Although thirst is a reliable sign that you need more hydration, you may need it even if you don't feel thirsty — so make it a habit of drinking water throughout the day.

Proper hydration is a critical factor in maintaining and improving your mind as you age. Dr. Daniel G. Amen explains, "Considering that your brain is 80 percent water, proper hydration is the first rule of good nutrition. Even slight dehydration increases the body's stress hormones, which can decrease your ability to think clearly. Over time, increased levels of stress hormones are associated with memory problems."

Alcohol and caffeine both have a dehydrating effect on your brain and body, so drink extra water in proportion to your enjoyment of wine and coffee. Avoid drinking anything that contains artificial sweeteners, added sugar, or chemical additives. Pure water is the best liquid to drink throughout the day, every day.

YOU ARE WHAT YOU DRINK

You are not just what you eat; you are also what you drink, according to Fereydoon Batmanghelidj, MD, a medical evangelist for the healing power of water. In his book *Your Body's Many Cries for Water*, he emphasizes that the quantity and quality of water that we drink have a profound effect on our health. Dr. Batmanghelidj has identified a common syndrome that he terms unintentional chronic dehydration (UCD). He believes that many ailments, such as headaches, arthritis, fatigue, constipation, and ulcers, are caused or exacerbated by UCD.

2. Starting Your Day with Breakfast

It is essential, after fasting overnight, to stimulate your metabolism by eating a healthy breakfast every morning. People who eat breakfast do a much better job of regulating their weight. According to a survey by the U.S. National Weight Control Registry, 80 percent of successful dieters, those who have lost weight and kept it off, ate breakfast daily. The survey concludes that "eating breakfast is a characteristic common to successful weight loss maintainers and may be a factor in their success."

In addition to helping prevent obesity, a healthy breakfast also has a positive effect on performance in memory tests, according to a study by researchers from the University of Toronto. They discovered that elderly men and women who ate breakfast scored significantly higher on tests of recall than those who skipped the morning meal. David Benton, PhD, of the University of Wales and his colleagues found the same phenomenon with schoolchildren. His research demonstrated that children who ate breakfast scored higher on memory tests and reported better moods.

Let food be your medicine.

— HIPPOCRATES

Neuroscientist Valerie Gremillion, PhD, confirms that "Breakfast establishes the core support for your brain function throughout the day and creates the conditions for enhanced mood, attitude, and motivation." You can optimize your brain functioning and your overall health by starting your day with fresh fruits, whole grains, and proteins: a bowl of berries or a grapefruit and steel-cut oats, or poached eggs and whole-grain toast, will do much more to satisfy your hunger and energize you for the day ahead than Pop-Tarts or Lucky Charms.

3. Rustproofing Your Brain and Body

If you leave a bottle of wine open too long, it will oxidize and become stale. If your car hasn't received the appropriate protective coating, it may rust over time. Just as wine degrades and metal rusts, so it is with the brain and body. Over the years, your system generates chemicals known as free radicals that have the effect of oxidizing, or "rusting," your cells.

FREE RADICALS

The Free Radical is the title of a libertarian journal published in New Zealand, and "the Free Radicals" also seems to be a popular name for rock bands, adopted by musicians in Texas, Florida, New Jersey, and elsewhere. But scientifically, the term doesn't refer to politics or music. Rather, it refers to unstable molecules — bereft of a needed electron — that roam around your system seeking to grab an electron from healthy molecules in order to stabilize themselves. Stealing an electron from a previously stable molecule makes that second molecule unstable, which then avidly seeks stabilization, thus perpetuating a chain reaction of molecular destruction that exacerbates symptoms associated with unhealthy aging.

Free-radical scavengers, known as antioxidants, can counter the destructive effects of free radicals by effectively quenching their desire for additional electrons, thus rendering them quiescent. Nutritionists at the National Institute on Aging in Bethesda, Maryland, have created a rating scale for the antioxidant level of various foods according to "oxygen radical absorption capacity," or ORAC. Enjoy foods with high ORAC ratings for the greatest "rustproofing" effect. The following are some delicious recommendations.

- *Live a fruitful life.* Raspberries, blackberries, straw-berries, and especially blueberries — which nu-tritionists have nicknamed "brainberries" — all have strong antioxidant benefits. Other fruits that serve as free-radical scavengers include pears, ap-ples, peaches, pomegranates, oranges, plums, kiwis, grapefruit, and red grapes. (Red grapes contain high levels of the potent antioxidants resveratrol and quercetin. This is partly why moderate enjoyment of red wine can be beneficial for your health.) Dried fruits, including prunes, dates, and apricots, can also be high in antioxidants. Check the labels before you buy dried fruits to be sure there are no preservatives, added sugar, or other unnecessary additives.
- *Veg out.* Broccoli, cabbage, cauliflower, brussels sprouts, spinach, kale, chard, carrots, chili peppers, bell peppers, parsley, asparagus, avocados, radishes, zucchini, beets, peas, seaweed, and artichokes con-tain a variety of wonderfully effective antioxidant components. The antioxidant benefits of these vege-tables are usually enhanced by cooking. A review, by Gladys Block, PhD, and her associates, of more than two hundred nutritional studies concluded that those who regularly ate more vegetables and fruit than average were significantly less vulnerable to cancer and heart disease.
- *Add garlic.* Garlic is one of the most healthful ingredi-ents you can enjoy in your daily diet. Garlic's benefits as an antioxidant, antibacterial, antifungal (and anti-vampiric) agent are well documented. It also helps

to maintain healthy cholesterol levels, reduce blood pressure, and promote good circulation.

- *Eat beans.* Although, as Bart Simpson informs us, "beans are neither fruit nor musical," they are high in antioxidants and fiber. Among the best are black, red, broad, kidney, and pinto.

- *Go nuts (and seeds).* Nuts and seeds are another rich source of antioxidants, especially pistachios, almonds, pecans, walnuts, hazelnuts, and sunflower seeds.

- *Add spices (and herbs) to your life.* These spices and herbs add more than flavor to your food, and they all offer a powerful antioxidant effect: cumin, cloves, cinnamon, turmeric, mustard, ginger, oregano, basil, sage, thyme, and tarragon.

- *Experience wholeness (through grains and cereals).* Barley, millet, oats, and corn are all loaded with vitamin E, a powerful antioxidant that helps prevent cancer by supporting the immune system. Studies also suggest that vitamin E helps prevent arthritis and may lessen the likelihood of Alzheimer's. A recent report from an American Society for Nutrition symposium states, "Current scientific evidence indicates that whole grains play an important role in lowering the risk of chronic diseases, such as coronary heart disease, diabetes, and cancer, and also contribute to body weight management and gastrointestinal health."

- *Enjoy teatime.* The world's most popular drink is also one of the healthiest. White, green, and black teas are all rich in antioxidants. Regular enjoyment of tea is a simple and refreshing way to help ward off a wide range of degenerative ailments, such as arthritis and Alzheimer's.

4. Minimizing or Eliminating the Unnecessary

In the Hippocratic oath, physicians swear to "first, do no harm." This is an essential principle of maintaining the health of your mind and body. Be careful to do no harm to yourself through eating useless or toxic substances. Some of the most common unnecessary elements to minimize or eliminate include sugar, saturated fats and "Frankenfats," high-glycemic carbohydrates, processed foods, additives, and preservatives.

The wisdom of life consists in the elimination of non-essentials.

— LIN YUTANG, Chinese author and inventor

Eliminate Unnecessary Sugar

Americans consume an average of 150 pounds of sugar per person per year, according to *Suicide by Sugar*, coauthored by clinical nutritionist Nancy Appleton. That book explains how overconsumption of sugar contributes to many disorders, from obesity and diabetes to depression and Alzheimer's. An overdose of sugar raises insulin levels in a way that can suppress the immune system, thereby increasing vulnerability to these and other ailments. Excess sugar also feeds inflammation throughout your body. Eliminating unnecessary sugar is difficult because it is a stealth ingredient in many foods, including a surprising number of so-called health foods. A recent trip to a natural foods store revealed "concentrated cane juice" (that is, sugar) in products ranging from chicken broth and frozen pizza to flaxseed waffles and beets. Is it necessary to artificially sweeten chicken broth? Do beets, naturally sweet, need to be treated with more sugar?

Here are some common aliases for unnecessary sugar:

- Corn syrup
- Cane juice
- Glucose
- Fructose
- Maltodextrin
- Malt syrup
- Sorbitol

Unnecessary sugar dulls your palate and contributes wasted calories to your diet. It is one reason that obesity is increasingly widespread. You will need to be vigilant to eliminate this unhealthy influence from your diet.

Tereza Hubkova, MD, an expert in healthy aging and a physician at the renowned Canyon Ranch Health Resort, explains, "Glucose (sugar) binds to the proteins in our arteries (and elsewhere) creating something called advanced glycosylated end-products — the abbreviation for which is AGE. This pretty much sums up what excess sugar does to your organs, including the brain."

THE SWEET SPOT FOR HEALTHY AGING?

Cynthia Kenyon, PhD, of the University of California, San Francisco, has discovered that lowering the amount of high-glycemic carbohydrates in one's diet may be key to a longer, healthier life. Working with a type of roundworm, Dr. Kenyon and her team found that when they fed their *C. elegans* roundworms sugar, it shortened their lifespan by revving up their insulin signaling system. Although Kenyon cautions that the research isn't yet conclusive, she has changed her own diet based on her discoveries. She explains, "Carbohydrates, and especially refined ones like sugar, make you produce lots of extra insulin. I've been keeping my intake really low ever since I discovered this. I've cut out all starch such as potatoes, noodles, rice, bread and pasta....Instead I have salads, but no sweet dressing, lots of olive oil and nuts, tons of green vegetables along with cheese, chicken, meat, fish and eggs. I eat some fruit every day, but not too much and almost no processed food. I stay away from sweets, except 80 percent chocolate." She adds that she enjoys "one glass of red wine a day."

Minimize Saturated Fats and Completely Eliminate "Frankenfats"

If you weren't a "fathead," you couldn't function. More than half of your brain's weight is fat, and without fatty acids, your neurons couldn't form or maintain synaptic connections. Healthy fats include the monounsaturated fats derived from olive oil, nuts (pistachios and almonds), and avocados, and the polyunsaturated fats sourced from some types of fish (salmon and mackerel) and from corn and safflower oils.

Saturated fats — found, for example, in red meat, egg yolks, butter, and cream — can contribute to the formation of plaque in the bloodstream and a subsequent hardening of the arteries. Foods with saturated fat can be enjoyed in moderation by most people who live a healthy lifestyle (including regular exercise) without significant negative consequences.

Trans fats, also known as "Frankenfats," are to be avoided completely. Just as Dr. Frankenstein artificially created a hideous monster, so food manufacturers have created artificial fats that have a monstrous effect on your health. Nutritionist Deborah Gleason explains how trans fats can contribute to depression and other mood disorders: "[They] interfere with the metabolism of essential fatty acids, and replace them in the cell membranes. When this occurs, various neurotransmitters responsible for mood, focus and memory have difficulty finding and identifying their receptors due to the distortion of the membranes on the receiving brain cells caused by the incorporation of trans fats." She adds that "trans fats are the primary villain (with a few runner-ups) that has created our epidemics of obesity, metabolic disorder, insulin resistance, and type 2 diabetes."

Also known as partially hydrogenated oils, trans fats are prevalent in margarine and other forms of shortening and present in many snack foods, such as chips, cookies, energy bars, crackers, peanut butter products, and breads. According to the Institute of Medicine, "There is no safe amount of trans fats in the diet."

OLIVE OIL: A GIFT FROM THE GODS

Good oil, like good wine, is a gift from the gods.
The grape and the olive are among the priceless benefactions
of the soil, and were destined, each in its way,
to promote the welfare of man.

—— GEORGE ELLWANGER, in *Pleasures of the Table*

One simple, delicious, and healthy change you can make in your diet is to use extra-virgin olive oil instead of butter, other animal fats, or partially hydrogenated oils. Extensive research shows that rates of cancer and heart disease are significantly lower in Spain, Greece, and Italy, and daily use of olive oil appears to be one of the main reasons, along with higher consumption of vegetables and fruits and moderate enjoyment of red wine with dinner.

Minimize High-Glycemic Carbohydrates

With most things in life, simplicity is better than complexity, but not in the world of carbohydrates ("carbs"). Complex (low-glycemic) carbs, such as those found in whole grains, beans, vegetables, and fruits, are much better for you than simple (high-glycemic) carbs, such as those found in soft drinks, candies, and bread, cakes, and cookies made from refined white flour. Derived from the Greek *glykeros* (sweet), *glycemic* means "having to do with the level of glucose [sugar] in the blood." Simple carbs are also known as high-glycemic because they can cause a sudden elevation of your blood sugar, followed shortly thereafter by a precipitous drop. This lowers energy, promotes weight gain, and contributes to a wide range of chronic ailments.

Low-glycemic foods, like beans, whole grains, and most vegetables, are integrated into your bloodstream more slowly than high-glycemic foods, such as Snickers, Twinkies, and Wonder bread. A low-glycemic diet facilitates a more regular pace of digestion, resulting in a steadier flow of energy to the brain, which optimizes your mental performance. Best of all, as Hyla Cass, MD, points out, low-glycemic meals are more satisfying.

CHECK YOUR GQ!

You can monitor your glycemic quotient (GQ) by learning about the effect of various foods on your blood sugar level at www.glycemicindex.com, which describes the Glycemic Index (GI). The GI categorizes carbs into three ranges: low (55 or less), medium (56–69), and high (70 and above). The higher the number, the more dramatic the alteration of your blood sugar.

Natural Highs: Supplements, Nutrition, and Mind-Body Techniques to Help You Feel Good All the Time, by Hyla Cass and Patrick Holford, offers wise advice in utilizing the GI: "Although it's very useful in helping us avoid high-glycemic villains, it's important to factor in a food's nutritional component along with its GI." Cass and Holford add, "While carrots, raisins, and bananas are relatively high on the GI, we don't recommend that you avoid these nutritious and delicious foods. No one ever got too fat from eating these foods. So defer to your common sense and use the GI as a guide, not your bible!"

Minimize Processing, Additives, and Preservatives

Leonardo da Vinci advised his students that simplicity was the essence of sophistication. This is particularly true when it comes to diet. Leonardo advocated eating the freshest food available. Eating unprocessed, additive-free food was relatively easy in Renaissance Italy, but it requires considerable sophistication now.

Although some preservatives and additives aren't harmful, many are unnecessary. And common sense dictates that fresher, unprocessed food will impart more vitality. Whenever possible, eat food that is minimally processed and free from additives, artificial ingredients, and preservatives. The simplest way to do this is to look for food that is marked "certified organic." (The Center for Science in the Public Interest offers a review of the safety of various preservatives on their website: www.cspinet.org/reports /chemcuisine.htm.)

> *Don't eat anything your great-great grandmother wouldn't recognize as food.*
>
> — MICHAEL POLLAN, author of *The Omnivore's Dilemma*

CAUTION! HIDDEN FOOD ALLERGIES

In the late 1950s, no one seemed to be aware that monosodium glutamate (MSG) — a flavor enhancer used in many Chinese restaurants — was the cause of a common food allergy. Today, most Chinese restaurants advertise that their food contains no MSG.

continued on the next page

Just as MSG was a hidden cause of a common food allergy, many of us suffer from allergic reactions to substances without realizing it. These hidden allergies can cause a range of problems, including digestive disorders, headaches or migraines, exacerbation of joint pain, breathing and sinus problems, and disturbances of mood.

Common food allergens include aspartame, dyes and food colorings, tree nuts, peanuts, milk, eggs, soy, shellfish, corn, wheat, gluten, tomatoes, and sugar. If you suspect that you may be allergic to a particular food, you can experiment by eliminating it from your diet for six weeks. If you have a reaction to it when you resume consumption, you will have confirmed the allergy.

Many physicians have discovered that the conditions of adults and children with emotional, learning, or behavioral problems will improve when they eliminate particular foods from their diets. As Dr. Daniel G. Amen comments, "My patients are often amazed that diet can make so much of a difference in their lives. By making simple changes to your eating habits, you too can improve brain function and improve your life."

5. Supplementing for a Sharper Mind

Can the appropriate use of supplements make you younger? Yes! According to Michael F. Roizen, MD, "The right nutrients in the proper amounts help protect your body from needless aging." For many years, the American Medical Association's official position was that vitamin supplementation was unnecessary for healthy adults. But they've since changed their stance and now advocate daily multivitamins to promote general health and prevent a range of chronic ailments. A report in the *New England Journal of Medicine* stated, "The evidence suggests that people who take [multivitamin and mineral] supplements and their children are healthier." In a study published in the medical journal the *Lancet*, ninety students were assigned to one of three groups: one received a multivitamin and mineral supplement; the second, an identical-looking placebo; and the third, nothing. After seven months, the IQ of those taking the supplements had increased by 9 points!

Some still contend that supplementation isn't necessary if one consumes a balanced diet. As Mark Hyman, MD, explains in *The UltraMind Solution: Fix Your Broken Brain by Healing Your Body First*, you don't need to bother with a multivitamin if you "eat wild, fresh, organic, local, non-genetically modified food grown in virgin mineral- and nutrient-rich soils that has not been transported across vast distances and stored for months before being eaten...and work and live outside, breathe only fresh, unpolluted air, drink only pure, clean water, sleep nine hours a night, move your body every day, and are free from chronic stressors and exposure to environmental toxins."

So, as Dr. Hyman suggests, if you don't live in Eden, then you may benefit from a high-quality daily multivitamin and mineral supplement. You may also wish to consider further supplementation, including the following.

• *Swallow some sunshine — additional vitamin D.* Our bodies produce vitamin D in response to sunshine, but most people don't get adequate daily sun exposure, especially in the winter. Vitamin D is essential for regulating the absorption of calcium and plays a significant role in bone health. Studies suggest that it may provide protection from osteoporosis, high blood pressure, a range of autoimmune conditions, and dementia.

- *Supersize the C.* High doses of vitamin C were championed by two-time Nobel Prize winner Linus Pauling in his controversial book *Vitamin C and the Common Cold.* Although the validity of Pauling's recommendations remains unproven, more recent studies, such as one published in *Seminars in Preventive and Alternative Medicine,* highlight the many benefits of vitamin C. The lead author, Mark Moyad of the University of Michigan, comments, "The more we study vitamin C, the better our understanding of how diverse it is in protecting our health." Moyad cites benefits including better visual acuity, strengthened immune function, and enhanced resistance to cancer and cardiovascular disease. Although controversy continues regarding the ideal dosage, the good news is that vitamin C is relatively safe. It may not be the cure for the common cold, but vitamin C supplementation has many proven benefits.

- *Go fish! Omega-3s.* Daily fish oil supplementation is another consensus "no-brainer" for the well-being of your brain. Pharmaceutical-grade fish oil, free from mercury and other toxins, provides the omega-3 fatty acids that are essential for your health. Fish oil helps to strengthen your immune system, improves your circulation, and counters inflammation in a way that can provide relief for arthritis and joint pain. Rich in DMAE, a nutrient that supports the important memory neurotransmitter acetylcholine, as well as in the essential fatty acids eicosapentaenoic acid (EPA) and docosahexaenoic acid (DHA), fish oil also has proven benefits in preventing depression, stabilizing mood, and promoting alertness. (Most of the studies that have demonstrated the benefits of fish oil utilize daily doses of 1000 mg and up.)

- *Further rustproofing.* In addition to eating plenty of high-ORAC foods, you may consider antioxidant supplementation. Some of the most potent "rust-proofers" include extracts of green tea, grape seed, resveratrol, and coenzyme Q_{10}, or CoQ_{10} for short. Also known as ubiquinol (because it is ubiquitous, that is, present in every cell), CoQ_{10} is a powerful antioxidant that works in concert with other nutrients to improve the functioning of all the cells of the body.

- *Brush up with extra fiber.* High-fiber foods such as vegetables, whole grains, beans, and fruits all serve to facilitate regularity by "scrubbing" your intestines. Also known as "roughage" or "bulk," dietary fiber helps to moderate blood sugar levels while reducing "bad" cholesterol (low-density lipoprotein, or LDL). For extra brushing power, you can supplement your diet with psyllium or flaxseeds.

- *Microbial reinforcements — probiotics.* Under normal conditions, our guts are teeming with healthy microorganisms that serve to promote digestion, nutrient absorption, and immune system functioning. Stress, dietary changes, intestinal infections, and many pharmaceuticals, especially antibiotics, can deplete our natural reserve of healthy microbes. Probiotics are supplementary live microorganisms (also known as "friendly bacteria") that shore up your natural intestinal microbial defense system. Live-culture yogurts, sauerkraut, kefir, and kimchi are all abundant sources of healthy bacteria. You can also take capsules with concentrated doses of these beneficial microorganisms.

The Mayo Clinic reports that many recent studies suggest probiotics are "effective in treating and possibly preventing diarrhea, caused by antibiotics or certain infections, or that occurs during travel." Researchers from Ohio State University and Virginia Tech found that probiotics may be useful in enhancing immune functioning, and a Swedish study suggests that probiotics may offer a number of benefits for promoting general health.

The following are some other potentially brain-boosting nutrients to consider.

• *Phosphatidylserine (PS)*. PS is a fat derived from lecithin. Studies show that PS may improve attention, concentration, mood, and short-term memory.
• *Ginkgo biloba*. The ginkgo tree is an ancient species, and its leaves have been used for centuries as a brain tonic. Ginkgo biloba may facilitate blood flow to the brain, resulting in an increase in alertness and an improvement of short-term memory. A large-scale study cast some doubt on the effectiveness of ginkgo biloba, but it continues to be a very popular and relatively safe supplement.

- *Turmeric.* A close relative of ginger, turmeric is a common ingredient in curry powder, known for its many therapeutic benefits. A study published in the *American Journal of Epidemiology* suggested that turmeric consumption helped to improve scores on a standard test of mental acuity in elderly subjects. Researchers from the Department of Neurology and Neurobiology of Aging at Kanazawa University in Japan report that turmeric "might be one of the most promising compounds for the development of [Alzheimer's disease] therapies," although they emphasize that further study is needed.

- *Acetyl-L-carnitine (ALC).* ALC is an amino acid that is "an important contributor to cellular energy metabolism," according to a study published in the *American Journal of Clinical Nutrition*. Working with subjects who were over one hundred years old, the researchers in this study discovered that ALC "facilitates an increased capacity for physical and cognitive activity by reducing fatigue and improving cognitive functions."

The right combination, timing, and dosage of supplements will depend on your age, gender, weight, and health. Also, be sure to keep in mind that the effectiveness of supplements is a function of the way they are absorbed by your system. That's one reason why higher-quality vitamins and minerals are often worth the investment. Consult a qualified health-care provider with special expertise in nutrition before taking supplements. A knowledgeable practitioner can help you discover the optimal combination that your body can absorb and utilize.

6. Embracing Moderation

The Greek philosopher Epicurus developed the philosophy of moderation. He explained, "No pleasure is a bad thing in itself, but the things which produce certain pleasures entail disturbances many times greater than the pleasures themselves." And he counseled, "Be moderate in order to taste the joys of life in abundance."

As Epicurus noted more than two thousand years ago, moderation is the key to the sustainable enjoyment of many of life's pleasures.

Good living is an act of intelligence, by which we choose things that have an agreeable taste rather than those which do not.

—JEAN ANTHELME BRILLAT-SAVARIN, French gastronomic philosopher

The good news is that a few of the most pleasurable, delicious treats are, when enjoyed in moderation, actually beneficial for your health. You'll get the most benefit from these treats if you seek out the highest possible quality and then focus your full attention on enjoyment.

Coffee: Sip Suave Molecules

A growing number of studies show that coffee has many significant health benefits, including lowering the risk of liver, prostate, and colon cancer, type 2 diabetes, and age-related mental decline. A study published in the *Journal of Alzheimer's Disease* found that people who regularly drank three to five cups of java daily were 65 percent less likely to suffer dementia later in life. And a report in the *European Journal of Clinical Nutrition* suggested that "consuming coffee reduces cognitive decline."

In 2011, Lyn Griffiths, PhD, director of the Griffith Health Institute in Brisbane, Australia, in collaboration with researchers from the University of Vienna, Austria, reported the results of a study on the health effects of regular, moderate coffee consumption. Sixty-two people took part in the trial, drinking three freshly brewed 250 ml cups of coffee per day for four weeks. After analyzing blood samples and comparing them to those of a non-coffee-drinking control group, the researchers concluded, "Coffee appears to have a protective effect in most people and provided a person's coffee consumption stays at a reasonable level, it can boost the self-defense system and fight carcinogens and toxins."

Of course, the caffeine in coffee can contribute to dehydration, and drinking it late in the day can exacerbate insomnia. But the potential benefits seem to outweigh the drawbacks. (Pregnant women and nursing mothers should consult a physician before consuming coffee, as some studies have demonstrated potential health risks for both mother and baby.)

Suave molecules of Mocha stir up your blood, without causing excess heat; the organ of thought receives from it a feeling of sympathy; work becomes easier and you will sit down without distress to your principal repast which will restore your body and afford you a calm, delicious night.

— PRINCE TALLEYRAND, French diplomat and bon vivant

Coffee stimulates circulation and elevates the levels of the neurotransmitter dopamine, an important regulator of mood. And it's packed with antioxidants. In a presentation to the American Chemical Society Joe Vinson, PhD, reported that Americans get more antioxidants from coffee than any other source.

Tomas DePaulis, PhD, a research scientist at Vanderbilt University's Institute for Coffee Studies, explains, "Overall, the research shows that coffee is far more healthful than it is harmful."

Chocolate: Health Benefits and Romance

Eating dark chocolate can raise alertness and temporarily improve performance in a range of cognitive tasks, according to a presentation given to the American Association for the Advancement of Science by Ian MacDonald, PhD. MacDonald's report is one of an increasing number of scientific studies demonstrating the benefits of moderate consumption of high-quality dark chocolate.

An article coauthored by Eric L. Ding, PhD, an epidemiologist and nutritionist with Harvard Medical School, summarized the results of twenty-one studies with a total of more than 2,500 participants, noting, "The large body of evidence from laboratory findings and randomized trials suggests that high flavonoid chocolate may protect against LDL oxidation, inhibit platelet aggregation, improve endothelial function, increase HDL (aka good cholesterol), lower blood pressure, and reduce inflammation — thereby protecting against the risk of cardiovascular disease."

Physicians from the Stockholm Heart Epidemiology Program discovered that chocolate may even be helpful in recovering from acute cardiovascular illness. They reported that twice-weekly consumption of high-quality dark chocolate lowered the risk of death following a heart attack by 66 percent.

Flavonoids, the ingredients responsible for these benefits, are also found in green tea, blueberries, and red wine.

In addition to these health benefits, chocolate is a reliable source of enjoyment. Dark chocolate induces the release of endorphins, which are associated with feelings of pleasure; it also contains serotonin, a chemical that acts as an antidepressant. Perhaps that's why chocolate lovers often experience chocolate as a substitute for (or complement to) romance.

Contemporary science seems to be confirming the benefits long suspected by epicures. The legendary gastronome Brillat-Savarin noted, "It has been shown as proof positive that carefully prepared chocolate is as healthful a food as it is pleasant; that it is nourishing and easily digested...that it is above all helpful to people who must do a great deal of mental work."

Red Wine: The Healing Power of the Grape

Curtis Ellison, MD, an epidemiologist and a wine lover, has devoted considerable time and energy to reviewing the literature on the health effects of wine. He told *Wine Spectator* magazine, "Moderate wine consumption can safely add pleasure to life. More significantly, it can also reduce our risks of falling prey to many of the most common health hazards of contemporary life, including heart disease, stroke, dementia, and even obesity. On balance, I believe moderate wine consumption can be a vital element of a lifestyle that will help us lead longer, healthier lives."

Researchers have conducted many studies on the potential health benefits of wine that support Dr. Ellison's optimism. The most reliable and significant findings all focus on the potential benefits of regular, moderate consumption of red wine to help reduce the risk of prostate and other forms of cancer, decrease the incidence of type 2 diabetes, avoid cardiovascular and coronary disease, and prevent Alzheimer's and other forms of dementia. Other benefits may include inhibiting the formation of peptic ulcers and reducing the risk of stroke, cataracts, anemia, tooth decay, and even the common cold.

Behold the rain which descends from heaven upon our vineyards; there it enters the roots of the vines, to be changed into wine, a constant proof that God loves us, and loves to see us happy.

— BENJAMIN FRANKLIN

In an article entitled "The Healing Power of Wine," *Wine Spectator* concludes, "So the question is no longer whether moderate consumption of wine is healthy, but why and how." Unlike beer or hard liquor, wine has always been appreciated as the beverage of moderation. Why? Because wine is designed to go with food and to be consumed slowly so that it can be fully appreciated. Drunkenness and alcoholism tend to be less common in Italy, Spain, and France, where children grow up with wine at the table. As the British author Thomas Walker noted more than two hundred years ago, "The art in using wine is to produce the greatest possible quantity of present gladness, without any future depression."

BRUSH AND FLOSS TO LIVE LONGER

Wine and coffee can discolor tooth enamel, but good dental hygiene is more than just a cosmetic issue — it's a frequently forgotten factor in healthy aging. A growing body

continued on the next page

of scientific evidence shows that many health challenges can be prevented through diligent oral care. Michael F. Roizen, MD, and Mehmet C. Oz, MD — authors of the phenomenal bestseller *YOU: Staying Young; The Owner's Manual for Extending Your Warranty* — were asked about the simplest, most surprising way their readers could help themselves stay young. Their answer: daily flossing and toothbrushing along with regular dental checkups. Roizen and Oz emphasize, "You won't just save your teeth; you'll also go a long way in saving your heart and arteries."

7. Enjoying Dining

Dining can be life's most reliable pleasure, but it also can become a burden when we worry about it. The French philosopher Voltaire observed, "Nothing would be more tiresome than eating and drinking if God had not made them a pleasure as well as a necessity." It's important to eat a healthy diet — avoiding the unnecessary and enjoying the fresh and wholesome — but it's equally important to relax and enjoy the pleasure of dining without obsessing about every calorie.

He who distinguishes the true savor of his food can never be a glutton; he who does not cannot be otherwise.

— HENRY DAVID THOREAU

As many have learned, "Dieting is not a piece of cake." Maintaining a healthy weight and percentage of body fat is critical to your long-term well-being, but if you are anxious about every calorie you consume, the anxiety may do you more harm than the calories. According to an article by Janet A. Tomiyama and her colleagues, "The attempt to cut calories often results in an increase in the stress hormone that is linked to the accumulation of excess belly fat."

Researchers estimate that almost 50 percent of American adults are, at any given time, attempting to lose weight, and the most common strategy is calorie counting and restriction, otherwise known as dieting. But the stress involved in this approach feeds a vicious cycle that helps us understand why most of those efforts fail. Studies show that most calorie counters gain back more weight than they lose!

The best way to regulate your weight and body fat percentage is to embrace a healthy lifestyle that includes mindful dining and regular exercise. Mindful dining begins with a few basic questions you can ask yourself before eating:

- How hungry am I now? You can rate yourself on a scale of 1 (not hungry) to 10 (very hungry).
- What do I really want to eat now?
- How will I feel after eating?

These simple questions will help you align your food choices with your appetite.

Another aspect of mindful dining involves taking the time to savor the beauty and pleasure of your food, enjoying the colors, aromas, textures, and tastes of every dish. If you are mindful, then you will want to choose food that is more wholesome and truly delicious, and if you choose food of that nature, it becomes easier to be mindful. Finally, you will discover that savoring something that is wholesome and truly delicious is far more filling, and fulfilling, than mindlessly swallowing junk.

You can further cultivate mindfulness by pausing before you dine to experience a sense of gratitude. In addition to the spiritual benefits, gratitude inspires a positive physiological response that supports healthy digestion and metabolism.

Mindful dining is much easier when you are getting regular exercise. Regular exercise helps you to become more sensitive and attuned to your own body. As your sensitivity and awareness increase, it becomes easier to make wiser choices about what to eat.

David L. Katz, MD, director of the Prevention Research Center at Yale University School of Medicine, explains, "By eating foods of higher overall nutritional quality, fullness can generally be achieved on fewer calories, eliminating the need for deprivation. In addition, physical activity can accelerate weight loss, promote health and alleviate stress in the bargain." Dr. Katz affirms that "eating well and being active for life is the way to go."

WHAT'S THE BEST DIET?

Should you "Eat Right for Your Type" or adopt the findings of "The China Study" and become a vegan like Bill Clinton? "The Paleo Diet" advocates a regimen based on the dining habits of our Paleolithic ancestors (lean meat, fish, fruits, nuts, and vegetables) and "Volumetrics" emphasizes healthy foods that give you a feeling of fullness. You can follow a diet named after a place: South Beach, Beverly

Hills, Sonoma, or Shangri-La; a doctor: Atkins, Perricone, Pritikin, Weil, or "Phil"; or a length of time: 3, 4, and 17 days are among the most popular at the moment.

What's the next major diet trend likely to be? A study by researchers at the University of Copenhagen published in the journal *Nature* suggests that humans can be categorized, regardless of ethnicity, gender, or age, into three "enterotypes." What's an enterotype? It's a characteristic pattern of bacteria in the gut. Your pattern of intestinal bugs may make it easier for you to extract nutrients from different types of foods. Look for some variation of the Bug Type Diet.

While you are figuring out the perfect eating plan, we can wholeheartedly recommend drinking plenty of pure water and eating a healthy breakfast every day to get off to a great start. Seek out fresh, wholesome, and vital foods. Your brain and body will thrive with plenty of "rustproofing," and you'll be healthier and happier as you minimize sugar, high-glycemic carbs, preservatives, and additives and eliminate "junk food" and trans fats. Consult with a health care provider who is knowledgeable about supplementation and practice moderation in all things, including your enjoyment of some of life's treats, such as coffee, chocolate, and wine.

Of the more than 90 billion people who have ever inhabited the earth, unless you are an identical twin, you possess DNA that is entirely unique. The ultimate diet plan involves tuning in to yourself and noticing how different foods affect you. If you practice mindfulness, self-awareness, and gratitude in your approach to dining every day you'll optimize your health and enjoyment and support the improvement of your mind as you age.

CHAPTER FIVE

Create a Brain-Enhancing Environment

Every aspect of your environment stimulates your brain, for better or worse. The sights, sounds, textures, aromas, tastes, and other sensations that you experience every day serve as nourishment for your mind and spirit. Unfortunately, the default setting in most situations — from cubicled working environments to airports, government buildings, hospitals, and schools — offers the brain a steady diet of junk food.

The good news, as the great psychological pioneer William James reminds us, is that we can overcome the effects of a negative environment:

> *A man should hear a little music, read a little poetry, and see a fine picture every day of his life, in order that worldly cares may not obliterate the sense of the beautiful that God has implanted in the human soul.*
>
> — JOHANN WOLFGANG VON GOETHE

"Environment modifies life but does not govern life. The soul is stronger than its surroundings." James also writes, "Why should we think upon things that are lovely? Because thinking determines life."

THE SOUL IS STRONGER THAN ITS SURROUNDINGS

When you first see Alice Herz-Sommer, you might think she looks old — maybe in her early eighties. But when you discover that she is 107, you realize that she is a paragon of youthfulness. In her thirties, Alice was a renowned concert pianist enjoying a flourishing career in her native city of Prague and throughout Europe. But then she was imprisoned in a concentration camp by the Nazi regime. Alice survived the Holocaust, emigrated to Israel and then to London, and resumed her career.

She attributes her survival, longevity, and well-being to her optimism and her lifelong passion for music. Until age 97, Alice went to the pool every day to swim. Now, her main exercise comes at the piano, which she continues to play daily. At age 104, she released *A Garden of Eden in Hell*, a bestselling memoir that recounted her amazing story. In 2010, the BBC produced a television program celebrating her life, and a clip from the show went viral on YouTube. Alice receives visitors in her North London apartment every day, and it's obvious when you watch the clips of the interactions that the visitors are deeply inspired by their time in her presence. Alice muses, "When you are optimistic, when you are not complaining…everybody loves you." She adds, "Only when we are so old, only then we are aware of the beauty of life."

One of the simplest and most delightful things you can do to improve your mind as you age is to create a beautiful, positive, brain-enhancing environment. This is more than a purely aesthetic enterprise — the quality of your everyday environment can have a profound effect on your cognitive wiring. As neuroscientist Richard Restak, MD, says, "Throughout life, not just during the first few months, the brain's synaptic organization can be altered by the external environment."

Mark R. Rosenzweig, PhD, of the University of California, Berkeley, was one of the pioneering researchers who helped to establish the validity of the notion of neuroplasticity. In his classic experiments, Rosenzweig placed rats in different environments: stimulus deprived and stimulus rich. The stimulus-deprived group was kept in empty cages (the rodent equivalent of cubicles), while the stimulus-rich group was raised in a cage equipped with mazes, ramps, wheels, and ladders. After 105 days, the rats' brains showed dramatic differences: the brains of the stimulus-rich group were larger and demonstrated more complex synaptic connections than those of the stimulus-deprived group.

Dr. Rosenzweig's work has led to many other experiments aiming to measure the effect of environmental stimulation on the brain and attempts to determine which environmental factors have the most influence. With rats, it turns out that the most brain-enriching aspect was the opportunity to move about freely. A study by Rosenzweig and his colleagues states, "For each species there exists a set of species-specific experiences that are maximally enriching and maximally efficient in developing its brain."

So what are the maximally enriching and efficient experiences for *Homo sapiens*? We don't yet have definitive experimental results measuring the effect of various environments on human brains, but there are a number of simple, positive steps you can take to create a more brain-enhancing environment now.

Elements of a Brain-Enhancing Environment

Sound: Harmonize Your Day

The sounds you hear every day affect your brain and body for better and for worse. According to the Environmental Protection Agency, "Noise pollution adversely affects the lives of millions of people." Research demonstrates that noise — defined as unwanted sound — can contribute to a range of stress-related ailments, including high blood pressure, insomnia, heartburn, indigestion, ulcers, and a number of mood disorders and mental problems. Rates of hearing loss among younger people are rising as noise pollution — especially from repeated exposure to extremely loud music — becomes more prevalent.

Never lose an opportunity of seeing anything that is beautiful, for beauty is God's handwriting — a wayside sacrament. Welcome it in every fair face, in every fair sky, in every flower, and thank God for it as a cup of blessing.

— RALPH WALDO EMERSON

One simple but important step in making your environment more brain friendly is to reduce the brain-polluting effects of noise. And just as noise can have a detrimental effect on your mind and body, so harmonious sounds can affect you in a positive way. For example, in 1993, neuroscientist Gordon L. Shaw, PhD, of the University of California and experimental psychologist Frances H. Rauscher, PhD, of the University of Wisconsin published a paper in the journal *Nature* showing that students who listened to Mozart's Sonata for Two Pianos in D Major improved their scores on a spatial-reasoning test, while those who sat in silence, or listened to New Age music, showed no improvement. This phenomenon, known as the Mozart effect, has inspired considerable controversy and many claims about the potential benefits of listening to classical music, Mozart in particular.

Many informal studies have shown that plants seem to grow better when exposed to continuous loops of Mozart's music, leading vintners such as Tuscany's Carlo Cignozzi to serenade their vines. Some dairy farmers have discovered that cows produce more milk when Mozart's music is played, a phenomenon playfully dubbed the "Moozart effect." Furthermore, hospitals around the world report faster patient recovery rates and happier, more relaxed staff when they listen to Mozart and other classical music.

In a 2004 article, *New Scientist* reported on research that helps to illuminate the brain physiology behind the Mozart effect. Hong Hua Li, PhD, a geneticist at Stanford University, and Frances H. Rauscher discovered that rats performed better on learning and memory tests after listening to Mozart sonatas, compared with the control group, which listened to white noise. The rats that had listened to Mozart showed increased levels of brain chemicals associated with learning and memory, neural growth, and synaptic formation. Rauscher and her team are hoping that their research will lead to the development of specific music therapy for people suffering from neurodegenerative diseases.

In the meantime, do your best to eliminate noise pollution and make beautiful, inspiring music part of your daily diet of sensory impressions. As the German poet Berthold Auerbach put it, "Music washes away from the soul the dust of everyday life."

Light: Brighten Your Life

Two thousand years ago, the great Roman physician Aulus Cornelius Celsus wrote *De medicina*, a compendium of wisdom on preventive health. He counseled, "Live in rooms full of light." The Romans didn't have to worry about the disjointing effects of flickering fluorescent lights or the energy inefficiency of incandescent bulbs, and they probably got more natural sunlight exposure on a daily basis than we do today.

I think you might dispense with half your doctors if you would only consult Dr. Sun more.

— HENRY WARD BEECHER

Light has a profound effect on body and mind, and it's an important aspect of creating a brain-enhancing environment. Natural sunlight is, of course, the healthiest source of light. It contains a rainbow of wavelengths that influence your hormone production, metabolism, and biological clock. Without adequate sunlight, the immune system is weakened, and many people experience depression.

Whenever possible, get outside for at least thirty minutes of sunlight each day without sunglasses: 98 percent of the benefits of sunlight are transmitted through the eyes and 2 percent through the skin. Of course, indoor jobs and inclement weather can make it difficult to spend the requisite time catching rays. The best indoor alternative is to use full-spectrum lighting, a form of light that mimics the natural effects of the sun.

John N. Ott, author of *Health and Light*, conducted pioneering research into the benefits of full-spectrum light. A photobiologist who worked for the Walt Disney Company, Ott was asked to apply his expertise in time-lapse photography to create the images that animators would use to express the transformation of a pumpkin into Cinderella's carriage. Ott's biggest challenge was creating the right conditions to grow pumpkins indoors. He experimented with many different types of light until he discovered that pumpkins thrive when exposed to the full spectrum of light. In subsequent research, Ott showed that full-spectrum light is healthier for plants and animals, including humans, than incandescent or fluorescent light. Among his many studies, he documented improvements in student behavior and test scores when classrooms switched from standard fluorescent lighting to full-spectrum lighting.

Try full-spectrum lighting in your home and office. It

> *Come forth into the light of things,*
> *Let Nature be your teacher*
> — WILLIAM WORDSWORTH

creates a balance of brightness and contrast that makes it easier to read, focus, and pay attention.

Nature: Reconnect with the Earth

Poets and philosophers have always counseled people regarding the benefits of being in nature, and now science is catching up. In a study published in the journal *Psychological Science* in 2008, neuroscientist John Jonides, PhD, and his colleagues measured students' performance on tests of memory and attention before and after taking a walk. One group strolled through a beautiful arboretum near the campus of the University of Michigan, and the other walked in downtown Ann Arbor. The researchers discovered that those who walked in nature improved their test scores by 20 percent, while those who walked in the city showed no improvement (moreover, they reported a decline in perceived well-being). The researchers concluded, "In sum, we have shown that simple and brief interactions with nature can produce marked increases in cognitive control. To consider the availability of nature as merely an amenity fails to recognize the vital importance of nature in effective cognitive functioning."

If one way be better than another, you may be sure it is nature's way.

— ARISTOTLE

In another important illustration of the "vital importance of nature" for our well-being, Stephen T. Sinatra, MD, and his associates have documented the healing benefits of simply standing on the earth with bare feet. In their book *Earthing*, they explain that our modern lifestyle has disconnected us from the regulating effects of the earth's electromagnetic field. They argue that standing on the ground, barefoot, for half an hour a day can help restore "your body's natural internal electrical stability and rhythms, which in turn promote normal functioning of body systems." They believe that this rebalancing can ameliorate a range of common problems, including inflammation, pain, fatigue, stress, and insomnia. In the words of the poet and naturalist Henry David Thoreau, "Heaven is under our feet as well as over our heads."

Air and Aroma: Breathe Freely

Along with harmonious sound and full-spectrum light, fresh air is an essential element for the long-term health of your body and mind. We may not be able to directly influence the quality of outdoor air in the place we live, but we can influence the quality of indoor air. Healthy houseplants serve as wonderful air fresheners, but if you are in an environment with lots of dust, pollen, and pollutants, you may need more help. There are many commercially available air purifiers on the market that can be helpful, especially for reducing allergy symptoms. (ClearFlite air purifiers are one example. You can find information on them at www.air purifiers.com.)

In addition to purifying the air, you may also benefit from scenting it. Aromas have a strong effect on mood and memory. Aromatic essential oils derived from plants have been used for millennia to treat a wide range of conditions, but it is only in the past few decades that aromatherapy has been studied scientifically.

In the journal *Advances in Psychiatric Treatment*, Clive Holmes, MD, and Clive Ballard, MD, published a paper entitled "Aromatherapy in Dementia." Holmes and Ballard conducted a survey of a number of clinical trials comparing the effects of lavender and lemon balm with those of placebos. They concluded, "All of these studies demonstrated a significant impact on behavioral problems in patients with dementia, with negligible side-effects."

Aromatherapists recommend jasmine, lavender, and rose to help overcome stress, and lemon, peppermint, and rosemary to boost concentration and memory. Smell and memory are intimately linked.

Moviegoers, for example, remember the details of the shows they've seen up to 50 percent more effectively when the scent of popcorn is wafted into the air. Diane Ackerman, author of *A Natural History of the Senses*, reminds us, "Nothing is more memorable than a smell." As she says, "Smells detonate softly in our memory like poignant land mines."

Aesthetics: Nurture Your Soul with Beauty

One of secrets behind Leonardo da Vinci's unparalleled ability to see and create beauty was the multisensory, brain-enhancing environment in his studio. His musician friends played for him as he painted, he scented the air with his favorite aromas of rose and lavender, and, of course, he was surrounded by the exquisitely beautiful images that he painted.

Leonardo embraced a renaissance of the teachings of Plato, the father of Western philosophy, who counseled, "He who would proceed aright should begin in youth to visit beautiful forms." Plato explains that surrounding yourself with beauty serves to nurture the mind and enrich the soul.

Anyone who keeps the ability to see beauty never grows old.

— FRANZ KAFKA

YOUR BRAIN ON ART

The Walters Art Museum in Baltimore is conducting a research project in collaboration with Johns Hopkins University entitled "Beauty and the Brain: A Neural Approach to Aesthetics." The study aims to understand why the human brain is attracted to artwork. Neuroscientists hypothesize that the brain activates in a special way when we view compelling artwork. Gary Vikan, director of the Walters, comments, "The artist is intuitively a neuroscientist."

Here are a few simple things you can do to bring more beauty into your life every day.

- *Display beautiful images in your office, on your screen saver, and in your home.* Choose an artist or a theme and hang up posters or download images that inspire you. The brain responds to variety, so change your "art exhibitions" from time to time, to create more positive stimulation.
- *Keep fresh flowers at home and at work.* Flowers are

perfect expressions of divine art. Novelist Iris Murdoch reminds us, "People from a planet without flowers would think we must be mad with joy the whole time to have such things about us."

- *Use your creativity to enrich your sensory environment.* Since every brain is different, you will get the best results if you tailor your own brain-enhancing environment. Consider all aspects and all the senses, even the feel of the clothes you wear. Choose fabrics and colors that make you feel good.

In *Magic Trees of the Mind*, Marian Diamond and Janet Hopson explain, "It doesn't take money to create a climate for enchanted minds to grow. It just takes information, imagination, motivation, and effort."

BRAIN RULE #9

In his book *Brain Rules*, John Medina sets out a series of scientifically based "rules" on how the brain works and how we can improve brain function. Medina's Brain Rule #9 is "Stimulate more of the senses." His research shows that a multisensory environment improves memory and learning ability. He writes, "Those in multisensory environments always do better than those in unisensory environments. They have more recall with better resolution that lasts longer, evident even twenty years later."

CHAPTER SIX

Cultivate Healthy Relationships (and Stay Sexy!)

Beautiful music, aesthetically pleasing sights, enlivening aromas, and inspiring illumination all serve to create the human equivalent of a stimulus-rich environment. But there's another aspect of a brain-enhancing environment that is so important it deserves its own chapter. Cultivating healthy relationships is one of the most important elements of improving your mind as you age.

Those who love deeply never grow old; they may die of old age, but they die young.

— BENJAMIN FRANKLIN

Aristotle believed that human beings were, by nature, social animals. He noted, "Whosoever is delighted in solitude is either a wild beast or a god." Despite Aristotle's observation, solitude can be delightful when it's chosen; but when it's the only option, as it often is for older people, it can lead to loneliness, alienation, and a sense of disconnection.

In many traditional societies, older people were at the center of their community's social life. They were consulted for their wisdom on a range of matters, and they often presided at rituals and ceremonies. In our current culture, we tend to treat older people as obsolete and rarely make them the center of social gatherings.

As George Burns approached age one hundred, he quipped, "I'd be happy to go out with women my own age, but there aren't any left." Maintaining a rich social life as the years go by requires conscious effort and planning.

Many studies demonstrate the importance of vibrant social interaction to support healthy aging. The *American Journal of Public Health* reported on a study of more than two thousand older women conducted over four years. Participants were interviewed to determine the extent and liveliness of their social lives. The women were asked questions such as "How many people can you rely on for help?" and "How many people can you confide in?" Researchers also monitored the number of the participants' social visits, phone calls, emails, and other forms of social communication. The results? Women with more expansive social networks were at significantly less risk of cognitive decline. And those who engaged in meaningful daily interaction with family and friends were almost 50 percent less likely to develop dementia.

Valerie C. Crooks, DSW, director of the study, explains, "Whenever we have even the most basic exchange, we have to think about how to respond, and that stimulates the brain.

There are people who are outliers, who have two very close relationships and are fine cognitively. But people who have three or more relationships tend to do better." Crooks summarizes the findings this way: "If you are socially engaged, you are at lower risk of dementia."

Researchers from the Rush University Alzheimer's Disease Center in Chicago studied a group of eight hundred octogenarians. At the beginning of the study, the subjects were all free from symptoms of cognitive decline. The participants completed an assessment designed to measure their relative degree of social integration or alienation. Those who reported that they were lonely were more than twice as likely to develop symptoms of dementia over the four-year term of the study than those with richer social lives.

A strong, healthy network of relationships protects against more than just dementia. Studies have also demonstrated that strong social networks and support groups can help people recovering from a wide range of ailments. Stanford University's David Spiegel, MD, and his colleagues published a landmark paper in the medical journal *The Lancet* in 1989, reporting that women with breast cancer who participated in support groups experienced less pain and lived twice as long as those who didn't participate in such groups. Other studies have shown that people with more friends tend to live longer after surviving a heart attack than those without a supportive social network. And even though social interaction increases your exposure to all manner of microbes, there's considerable evidence that the immune-strengthening benefits of friendships outweigh the risks. People with more friends have fewer colds and re-cover faster when they do catch one.

Loneliness isn't just an issue for older people; it has become a pandemic in our society. In 2006, the *American Sociological Review* published a study showing that social isolation affects people of all ages and that it is more preva-lent now than ever before. Almost 25 percent of the subjects in this comprehensive research project reported that they had no one in whom to confide, a percentage that had more than doubled in the previous two decades.

John T. Cacioppo, PhD, a psychologist at the University of Chicago, has researched the relationship between social psychology and neuroscience for more than thirty years. In 2008, with coauthor William Patrick, Cacioppo published the groundbreaking book *Loneliness: Human Nature and the Need for Social Connection*. Cacioppo and Patrick make a powerful case that a healthy social network is a major determinant of overall mental health and physical well-being. Together they have pioneered the emerging disci-pline of social neuroscience. They argue that our brains are hardwired to thrive through social interaction and that, as Aristotle suggested, we experience grave stress in isolation. As Cacioppo and Patrick comment, "Our sociality is central to who we are."

Invest in Your Social Wealth

The best time to begin saving for your retirement is at the beginning of your career. Most people are aware of the importance of saving enough money so that they can live comfortably when they stop working. But what many people don't realize is the importance of investing in their social capital as well. John T. Cacioppo has coined the term "social wealth" to refer to the abundance of positive, healthy

My friends are my estate.

— EMILY DICKINSON

relationships that serve to nurture us in a variety of practical ways. A rich social life will help you avoid cognitive decline as it strengthens your immune system. Here are some simple, positive practices and principles for cultivating your social network.

- *Take classes.* Expand your social network by learning with others. When you learn chess, languages, tai chi, yoga, flower arranging, cooking, or investing along with others, you multiply the benefits.
- *Cherish friendships.* True friendships are rare and precious. When you identify current or potential true friends, do your best to cultivate and cherish the relationship. Thinking skills pioneer Tony Buzan and chess grandmaster Raymond Keene, in their extensive survey of the research into aging and the brain, concluded that having close friends increases longevity. And you'll discover that the benefits of close friendships multiply as the years go by. As Thomas Jefferson wrote, "I find friendship to be like wine, raw when new, ripened with age...the true restorative cordial....The happiest moments my heart knows are those in which it is pouring forth its affections to a few esteemed characters."

- *Take the social initiative.* Rather than waiting for invitations, take the initiative: invite potential friends for dinner or to a movie, concert, or lecture.
- *Dine with others.* As the Italians say, *A tavola non si invecchia* — "at the table, you don't grow old." Sharing a meal with others daily is one of the practices common to the world's longest-living people, according to Dan Buettner, author of *The Blue Zones: Lessons for Living Longer from the People Who've Lived the Longest.*
- *Volunteer.* Caring for others is one of the surest ways to feel better about yourself. Helping out at a soup kitchen, animal shelter, hospice, or school provides a sense of meaning and purpose that keeps you sharp and more fulfilled.
- *Mentor younger people.* Older people who provide intergenerational guidance experience profound benefits. A study by Elizabeth Larkin and her colleagues, published in the *Journal of Gerontological Social Work*, reports that "the mentoring experiences allow opportunities for older adults to renew positive emotions and reinforce meaning in their lives."
- *Surround yourself with positive people.* Socializing isn't automatically beneficial. It has to be fundamentally positive to yield brain benefits. Negative relationships characterized by whining, complaining, judgment, and abusive language can, according to some studies, be detrimental to our cognitive and emotional lives. You'll discover, however, that if you

embrace an optimistic, upbeat attitude, it becomes easier to meet other optimistic, upbeat people.

- *Continuously improve your listening skill.* Listening is like driving — most people think they are better than average, but, of course, that can't be true. The best listeners adopt an attitude of humility, empathy, and continuous improvement. As playwright Wilson Mizner observed, "A good listener is not only popular everywhere, but after a while he gets to know something."

Adopt a Pet

In a classic *Seinfeld* episode, Jerry observes, "People... they're the worst." If you concur but still want the brain benefits of socializing, the good news is that pets can provide similar effects.

After conducting health evaluations of almost 6,000 people, 784 of whom were pet owners, Warwick Anderson discovered that the pet owners had significantly healthier cholesterol counts and blood pressure readings. They also reported experiencing less stress. According to James Serpell, author of *In the Company of Animals: A Study of Human-Animal Relationships*, the benefits of caring for a pet are stronger than "the known effects of other positive lifestyle factors such as regular exercise or low-fat diets." He adds, "Pet owners

If all the beasts were gone, men would die from a great loneliness of spirit.

— CHIEF SEATTLE, in a letter to President Franklin Pierce

also reported improved psychological well-being and self-esteem scores compared with a group of non-owners."

Other studies demonstrate that the key to the brain benefits of pet ownership is the level of engagement with the pet. In other words, it's not enough just to have one; it's the process of caring, petting, and relating that yields the experience of well-being.

THE LOVE RESPONSE

Eva Selhub, MD, instructor in medicine at the Harvard Medical School, believes that cultivating healthy relationships is an essential element in improving your mental and physical health as you age. "I have found that a key factor for health is love," she says. "Love sets off a set of physiological events in the body that help you to adapt to life's challenges, to stop and reverse disease, to maintain health, and to make it easier for your body to improve rather than deteriorate with age."

Dr. Selhub notes that when you look into the eyes of someone you cherish, exchange hugs, enjoy sex, or just experience loving feelings, you raise the levels of oxytocin in your system. She explains, "Known as 'the love hormone,' oxytocin enhances social attachment, bonding, and other social behaviors. It reduces anxiety, fear, and activation of the stress response (including stress hormones like cortisol) while increasing relaxation and rewarding feelings such as peace and balance." In other words, the "Love Response" is the physiological counterpoint to the fight-or-flight response.

Stay Sexy!

If social interaction and touching are good for the aging brain, then sex must be golden. But sex in the golden years doesn't get much attention in popular culture. Despite the media's overemphasis on horny housewives, naughty politicians, and pubescent heartthrobs, many Americans over fifty enjoy sex lives that are lively and fulfilling.

In an analysis of the data from two different major studies of older Americans, researchers noted that the majority of subjects reported being sexually active in the preceding year. The most significant finding, however, was that *overall health, independent of age, was a significant indicator of the frequency and quality of sexual activity*. The study concluded, "Frequency of sexual activity, a good quality sex life, and interest in sex are positively associated with health in middle age and later life."

Having sex is like playing bridge. If you don't have a good partner, you'd better have a good hand.

— WOODY ALLEN

According to Walter M. Bortz, MD, fitness is a key to healthy sexuality, and healthy sexuality promotes fitness, in a virtuous cycle. In his book *Living Longer for Dummies*, Bortz says, "Sex can extend your life." He cites research demonstrating that satisfying sexual activity enhances both the quality and the duration of life. Bortz also encourages us to move beyond the negative stereotypes associated with sexuality and aging, arguing that our sexuality can continue to evolve, and even improve, as we age. He explains, "Aging brings advantages to sexuality....It is affirming...smarter, less urgent and more honest." Like fine wine, our sexuality can become more nuanced and profound as we age.

Secrets of a Happy Sex Life after Fifty

The following recommendations will improve your sex life after age fifty — and prior to age fifty as well!

Flirt

You don't actually have to engage in sex to stay sexy. Sexiness is a life-affirming attitude that you share with others, and flirting is a delightful way to cultivate it. Flirting, defined by *Webster's* as "to behave amorously without serious intent," is a way to share sensuality and sexuality without attachment, consequence, or guilt.

The older the fiddler, the sweeter the tune.

— English proverb

Develop Erotic Awareness: Savor All the Senses

You can expand your notion of sexuality by exploring the pleasure of sensual delights in everyday life, such as by

- Savoring the exquisite beauty of an orchid
- Luxuriating in the shower or bath
- Allowing a piece of fine dark chocolate to melt in your mouth
- Opening your heart as you listen to your favorite music
- Spending a full minute savoring the aroma of a glass of good wine

- Contemplating the dancing flames in your fireplace
- Laughing — Joanne Woodward, married happily to screen legend Paul Newman for fifty years, observed, "Sexiness wears thin after a while and beauty fades, but to be married to a man who makes you laugh every day — ah, now that's a real treat."

Don't Take Yourself Too Seriously

"Sex is God's joke on human beings," according to the inimitable femme fatale actress Bette Davis. In case you haven't noticed, the sex "act," and much of the behavior associated with it, is somewhat absurd. As we mature, it's easier to relax about the whole subject of dating and mating. Embrace a curious, lighthearted, open, and exploratory attitude about life in general and sex in particular. Life is an adventure, and sex is one of its more enchanting and vexing mysteries. As a female meteorologist observed, "Sex is like snow — you never know how many inches you're going to get or how long it will last."

Be Creative: Fulfill Erotic Wishes

You can spice up your sex life by using your creativity to delight your partner, thereby inspiring your partner to be more creative in pleasing you. You can stimulate creativity and exquisite pleasure with a game called Three Minutes in Heaven. The rules are simple: You and your partner agree to focus on each other's erotic wishes with complete attention for alternating three-minute periods. Begin by asking your partner what she or he would like you to do (besides "paint my house"!). Your partner might request: "Kiss my neck," "Massage my thighs," "Suck my toes." Do whatever your partner desires for three minutes with complete devotion and focus. When the time is up, you ask your partner for whatever you desire. Aim to play three rounds.

If you don't have a partner or don't want one, creativity is even more important. Explore the autoerotic realm. If you need some remedial help in this area, consult Betty Dodson's *Sex for One: The Joy of Selfloving*.

Stay Fit and Satisfied

Regular exercise and a healthy diet keep your mind sharp and enhance your sexual vitality. In a comprehensive study entitled "Sexual Desirability and Sexual Performance: Does Exercise and Fitness Really Matter?" Tina M. Penhollow, PhD, and Michael Young, PhD, of the University of Arkansas concluded, "Exercise frequency and physical fitness enhance attractiveness and increase energy levels, both of which make people feel better about themselves. Those who exercise are more likely to experience a greater level of satisfaction."

Embrace the Moment

Instead of thinking of orgasm as something to be "achieved" — like a promotion at work or a better score in golf — embrace the notion of mindfulness applied to intimacy. In other words, allow yourself to be fully present in the moment. Ironically, the more fully you embrace the moment, the deeper and richer the "results" become.

Peggy J. Kleinplatz, PhD, of the faculty of medicine at the University of Ottawa, one of the world's leading

HORMONES: KEEP YOUR VITAL FORCES MOVING

The word *hormone* is derived from the ancient Greek *horman*, translated as "to set in motion." Our hormones help to generate the motion of our vital forces. As we age, changes in hormonal levels can affect both men and women, causing symptoms ranging from depression and loss of libido to moodiness and difficulty sleeping.

A positive attitude, healthy diet, and regular exercise all help to regulate hormone balance. But sometimes these lifestyle practices are insufficient, and you may wish to consider hormone replacement therapy (HRT). When considering HRT, educate yourself on the subject. Avoid any product hyped as a cure-all. HRT has potential benefits and risks. Discuss HRT options with a physician who understands the complexities of clinical endocrinology.

researchers into human sexuality, explains that sexual fulfillment isn't a matter of exotic positions or sex toys. According to Kleinplatz and her colleagues, the most important factor is "being able to be fully absorbed in each other in the moment."

Change Your Metaphor

Many of us grew up with baseball as our metaphor for sex — "getting to second base" or "striking out." We love the national pastime, but after adolescence, you will probably be happier with metaphors that don't rely on competitive allusions. Instead, explore metaphors of confluence, such as those from the world of music: consider "making beautiful music together" and "harmonizing" with your partner.

Put Your Partner's Needs First, Then Clearly Express Yours

This is a general life principle that pays extra dividends in the bedroom. As the great Taoist philosopher Lao-tzu explains, "If you would take, you must first give; this is the beginning of intelligence."

ALWAYS FOLLOW MISS MANNERS'S DATING ADVICE!

According to Judith Martin, the author of *Miss Manners' Guide to Excruciatingly Correct Behavior:* "There are three possible parts to a date, of which at least two must be offered: entertainment, food, and affection. It is customary to begin a series of dates with a great deal of entertainment, a moderate amount of food, and the merest suggestion of affection. As the amount of affection increases, the entertainment can be reduced proportionately. When the affection is the entertainment, we no longer call it dating. Under no circumstances can the food be omitted."

Embrace Vulnerability, Authenticity, and Good Communication

A study published in the *Canadian Journal of Human Sexuality* concludes that comfort with vulnerability, authenticity, and good communication is the key to a wonderful sex life. Dr. Peggy J. Kleinplatz, the study's lead author, advises that we learn "to be emotionally naked while being seen by a partner." As we mature, it becomes easier to accept ourselves and view our partners with compassion. That's why we shouldn't be surprised that Kleinplatz's research shows that sexual fulfillment flourishes in relationships deepened with maturity. Kleinplatz states, "Sex gets surprisingly better with experience and becomes self-perpetuating....Aging may be an asset towards optimal sexual development." In her article "Why I'd Rather Sleep with an Old Guy," Katherine Anne Forsythe explains some of the reasons why sex with a mature partner can be satisfying: "Men over fifty, sixty, seventy-five, even ninety can be great lovers for three basic reasons. Primarily, they are not in a hurry. Secondly, they put their partner's needs first. Thirdly, they have learned that great sex doesn't have to include intercourse at all — it's only one option."

A heart that loves is always young.

— Greek proverb

CHAPTER SEVEN

Rest Peacefully to Delay Resting in Peace

The great virtuoso pianist Artur Schnabel commented, "The notes I handle no better than many pianists. But the pauses between the notes — ah, that is where the art resides!" Creating a brain-enhancing environment, learning new things, cultivating a vibrant social network, and implementing a program of exercise and diet are all positive actions you can take to improve your mind as you get older. And one of the most important aspects of healthy aging focuses more on the art of non-doing — the space "between the notes" of your positive actions. Understanding how to rest and recharge will help you to achieve greater health of body and mind.

> *It is sweet to let the mind unbend.*
>
> — HORACE,
> Roman poet

Sleep Well

How important is it to sleep well? "Sleep is as critical as food and oxygen," cautions Walter M. Bortz, MD. "Generally, we need eight hours a night. That is one of the most important determinants of how long people live."

Sleep is something that many folks take for granted, but since it takes up about one-third of our lives, it's worth considering carefully. Besides the obvious benefit of providing time for cell regeneration and repair, eight hours of regular, sound sleep sets you up for optimal functioning of mind and body. It strengthens your immune system, improves your mood, and sharpens your alertness and powers of attention. Getting sufficient sleep lowers your risk of high blood pressure, heart disease, obesity, and diabetes, and it makes you less susceptible to accidents.

Sleep also plays a critically important role in memory consolidation and creative thinking. Most people have experienced "sleeping on" a problem and awakening with greater clarity and insight about it. Robert Stickgold, PhD, of the Division of Sleep Medicine at Harvard Medical School is trying to understand why and how this happens. Stickgold notes, "The fundamental purpose of sleep is to catch up on processing information received during waking hours. Parts of the brain that do this are not available when you are awake; they are busy with other tasks." Or as Sigmund Freud expressed it in *The Interpretation of Dreams*, "The dream acts as a safety-valve for the over-burdened brain."

Guidelines for Sleeping Well

Comedian Steven Wright jests, "When I woke up this morning my girlfriend asked me, 'Did you sleep well?' I said, 'No, I made a few mistakes.'" Below is a simple guide to mistake-free sleep.

- *Darkness helps.* Darkness stimulates the production of the hormone melatonin, a key catalyst of sleep.
- *Quiet is best.* Sleeping through a noisy night can raise your blood pressure, even when you're unaware of it. You can use earplugs or white noise generators to block out disturbing sounds.

> *A well-spent day brings happy sleep.*
> — LEONARDO DA VINCI

- *Be cool.* A cooler temperature makes it easier to sleep. Keep your bedroom below seventy degrees Fahrenheit. (Take a hint from bears — they hibernate for up to seven months in caves that are dark, quiet, and cool.)
- *Find the right mattress.* Discover the level of support that works best for you. Also consider the sheets, pillows, and blankets that make you most comfortable. Many people find that they sleep better when they use all-cotton sheets and avoid synthetics.
- *Avoid caffeine after noon.* Caffeine can stay in your system, and keep you awake, for eight to twelve hours.
- *Exercise, but avoid vigorous exercise before bedtime.* Vigorous exercise will help you sleep better as long

as you don't do it within four hours of attempting to sleep.

- *Create rituals that help you relax.* A relaxing pre-bedtime bath, a spray of lavender scent, reading from an inspiring text, writing in a gratitude journal — these are just a few suggestions for helping you ease into a night of restful sleep. Create a ritual that works for you.

- *Try natural sleep aids.* If you have trouble falling asleep, you may wish to try some natural sleep en-hancers. Valerian is a sleep-inducing herb that many people find helpful. Melatonin supplements may help regulate your circadian rhythms. Other poten-tially useful supplements include magnesium citrate or magnesium glycinate, calcium, theanine (an amino acid from green tea), GABA (gamma-aminobutyric acid), 5-HTP (5-hydroxytryptophan), passionflower, and magnolia. The homeopathic formula Calms Forté can also work well without any side effects. (Consult your health-care practitioner to determine the sleep aid and dosage that are best for you.)

- *Keep a regular schedule.* Aim to keep a regular sleep schedule. Ideally, you go to sleep and wake up at the same times, but if you have to choose, put the em-phasis on the consistency of your waking time. This helps to regulate your internal body clock.

- *Listen to the Slow-Wave Sleep audio download in-cluded with this book.* It combines the soothing sound of ocean waves with delta waves to gently lull you to sleep.

THE POWER OF REST:
WHY SLEEP ALONE IS NOT ENOUGH

Matthew Edlund, MD, is the director of the Center for Circadian Medicine in Sarasota, Florida. Based on his extensive clinical research, Edlund discovered that many people are, as he describes it, "rest deprived." Although he offers excellent advice on sleeping well, Edlund emphasizes that sleep is just part of the larger spectrum of rest. Our systems are overloaded with stress, and our natural rhythms of rest and refreshment are obscured by the hectic pace of contemporary living. Edlund proposes that we relearn how to rest. The first step in doing this is to recognize that you will feel better and work more effectively if you are well rested. Edlund offers plenty of evidence to this effect, plus guidance on four essential dimensions of rest:

- *Physical rest.* In addition to sleep and naps, Edlund recommends soaking in a hot tub or relaxing in a yoga pose.
- *Mental rest.* Mental rest involves reconfiguring one's mind to quickly and easily obtain a sense of relaxed control. Edlund recommends self-hypnosis, relaxation exercises, and positive visualization.
- *Social rest.* Edlund explains that social rest involves "using the power of social connectedness to relax and rejuvenate." He highlights the fact that feelings of belonging and togetherness are essential for our well-being.
- *Spiritual rest.* Edlund recommends daily practice of meditation, prayer, and contemplation.

The Art of Napping

Thomas Edison filed for his 1,093rd patent (a record number) when he was eighty-three years old. Leonardo da Vinci created one of history's greatest masterpieces, the *Mona Lisa*, when he was in his fifties. Edison, da Vinci, and many other great geniuses all practiced the art of napping. As Frank Dyer and Thomas Martin explain in their biography of Edison, "[He] would use several volumes of *Watt's Dictionary of Chemistry* for a pillow, and we fellows used to say that he absorbed the contents during his nap, judging from the flow of new ideas he had on waking."

For centuries, we had only anecdotal evidence to affirm the value of napping, but contemporary science is now validating the practice. Harvard's Robert Stickgold explains, "[Napping] helps clear out the brain's 'inbox' and integrates that information into memory. During most of history, humans took siestas for this purpose. Modern men and women are perhaps the only advanced species of animal that goes 16 hours or more a day without a nap."

Think what a better world it would be if we all, the whole world, had cookies and milk about three o'clock every afternoon and then lay down on our blankies for a nap.

— ROBERT FULGHUM, author of *All I Really Need to Know I Learned in Kindergarten*

A strategic nap is an effective way to heighten alertness and enhance performance, according to Mark R. Rosekind, PhD, former director of NASA's Fatigue Countermeasures Program. Rosekind and his team found that aviators who took naps averaging twenty-six minutes improved their performance by up to 34 percent. He advises limiting naps to less than forty minutes to avoid grogginess, and most expert "napologists" also recommend napping prior to 5:00 PM to avoid interference with evening sleep.

In *Take a Nap! Change Your Life*, Sara C. Mednick, PhD, makes a compelling case for the benefits of napping. Her research demonstrates that in addition to raising alertness and improving your mood, naps can sharpen your memory and boost your creative problem-solving skills. A student of Robert Stickgold, Mednick confirmed through her work what Leonardo and Edison had both intuited: "Learning after a nap is equal to learning after a full night of sleep."

Meditate for Healthy Aging

Although the Dalai Lama advises that "sleep is the best meditation," His Holiness begins each day with four hours of meditation practice. But the Nobel Prize–winning monk and spiritual leader notes that just five minutes of daily meditation can have profound benefits. Contemporary science supports the Dalai Lama's contention.

"The effects of meditation can counter the effect of age," according to Sara W. Lazar, PhD, and her colleagues at Harvard Medical School. Their work has shown that meditation practice improves memory and concentration as well as correlating with positive physical changes in the thickness of the prefrontal cortex. Lazar

> *To the mind that is still, the whole universe surrenders.*
>
> — LAO-TZU,
> father of Taoism

and her colleagues state, "Our data suggest that meditation practice can promote cortical plasticity in adults in areas important for cognitive and emotional processing and well-being."

In 1982, Robert Keith Wallace, PhD, and his associates published their findings regarding the effects of meditation on aging in the *International Journal of Neuroscience*. They reported that subjects who had been practicing Transcendental Meditation for five years or more had a biological age averaging twelve years younger than their chronological age. In other words, a fifty-year-old meditator had the physiology of a thirty-eight-year-old.

Meditation Reduces Stress

Why does meditation offer such profound benefits? The answer, according to research, is that stress is the single greatest contributor to the symptoms associated with aging, and meditation is a powerful antidote. "If we can affect the stress response, we can affect the aging process," reports Eva Selhub, MD, an instructor of medicine at Harvard Medical School. "There's a reason why experienced meditators live so long and look so young."

Bernie S. Siegel, MD, author of *Love, Medicine and Miracles*, explains it this way: "Peace of mind sends the body a 'live' message, while depression, fear and unresolved conflict give it a 'die' message." Siegel additionally notes, "The physical benefits of meditation have recently been well documented by Western medical researchers....Meditation also raises the pain threshold and reduces one's biological age.... In short, it reduces wear and tear on both body and mind, helping people live longer and better."

Herbert Benson, MD, is one of the pioneers of mind-body medicine and a trailblazer in the scientific study of meditation. Benson, a cardiologist, published *The Relaxation Response* in 1975. In this groundbreaking book, Benson introduced the idea that meditation serves as an antidote to stress. He elucidated the nature of the fight-or-flight response and documented the ways in which the stresses of modern living tend to overactivate it. Benson studied a variety of approaches to meditation, searching for the elements that help to counter the effects of chronic stress. The genius of his work is in his focus on separating meditation practice from religious and cultural associations in an attempt to discover the elements that facilitate measurable physiological benefits.

Benson demonstrated that meditation creates conditions that are the opposite of the fight-or-flight response and bring about what he called the "Relaxation Response." He showed that meditation practice regulates blood pressure as it slows heart rate and respiration and that meditation serves as a concentrated form of rest and recovery.

You can evoke the relaxation response by following these simple directions:

- Sit quietly in an upright, comfortable position.
- Gently close your eyes.
- Scan your muscles — beginning with your feet and progressing up to the top of your head — and gently request that they relax.

- Bring your attention to your breathing (breathe through your nose, if possible). Keep your attention on the flow of breath, and as you exhale, say the word "one" silently to yourself.
- Breathe easily and naturally. Just silently repeat the word "one" with each exhalation.
- Continue for twenty minutes. (It's fine to open your eyes from time to time to peek at the clock; or just set a timer.)
- Avoid worrying about how well you did. As Woody Allen said, "90 percent of success is just showing up." This is especially true for meditation. If you just sit and maintain a receptive attitude, the relaxation response will take place. When your mind wanders, just return to the awareness of your breath and to the repetition of "one."
- For optimal results, practice twice a day. Avoid practicing after dining, as meditation is much easier on an empty stomach.

Meditation Relieves Pain and Improves Your Brain

Jon Kabat-Zinn, PhD, the founder and director of the Stress Reduction Clinic at the University of Massachusetts Medical Center, collaborated with Herbert Benson. His extensive studies on patients with chronic pain were featured on the PBS series *Healing and the Mind* with Bill Moyers. Kabat-Zinn's research has consistently demonstrated the value of meditation in reducing many kinds of pain, even for patients who were unresponsive to standard medical treatments.

Moreover, a study published in the journal *Psychiatry Research: Neuroimaging* in 2011 reports strong evidence that meditation can significantly change the structure of the brain. Britta K. Hölzel, PhD, and her colleagues discovered that meditating for just thirty minutes a day for eight weeks can increase the density of gray matter in brain regions associated with memory, stress, and empathy.

Hölzel and her team tracked sixteen novice meditators who were participating in Kabat-Zinn's Mindfulness-Based Stress Reduction (MBSR) program. For decades, participants in the MBSR program reported feeling less stress and more positive emotions. But in this study, the researchers weren't just asking the participants how they felt; they were examining the participants' brains — two weeks before and just after the eight-week program. Over the same period, they also scanned the brains of a control group, which didn't receive the meditation training.

You can download your complimentary audio program at www .brainpowerdownload.com (coupon code: MeditateMe). A CD can also be purchased at the same website.

The control group, as you might imagine, didn't show any changes in their brain structure. The brain scans of the MBSR meditators, who spent just half an hour per day meditating, showed that their gray matter had become significantly thicker in several regions. One of those regions, the hippocampus, is an area of the brain that is crucial for learning, memory, and the regulation of emotion.

MEDITATION BENEFITS

Regular meditation practice offers many measurable benefits. Specifically, meditation

- Helps oxygen to be utilized more efficiently
- Reduces the perception of pain
- Regulates blood pressure
- Deepens relaxation and reduces muscle tension
- Lowers levels of cortisol and other stress hormones
- Improves breathing for asthma patients
- Strengthens the immune system
- Helps alleviate headaches and migraines
- Reduces symptoms of premenstrual syndrome
- Facilitates faster postoperative recovery
- Supports emotional stability and resilience
- Relieves symptoms of anxiety and depression
- Increases feelings of happiness, contentment, and peace
- Improves memory and reaction time
- Develops coordination
- Enhances coherence of brain wave patterns that correlate with improvements in learning ability and creativity

CHAPTER EIGHT

Liberate Your Mind by Synchronizing Your Brain

Meditation is one of the most powerful means to improve your mind as you age. But some folks have trouble sitting still for any length of time. Others find that despite their best efforts, they aren't able to stop attending to distractions. What if you could utilize simple audio technology to ease your brain waves into patterns that are indistinguishable from those of someone who has practiced meditation for decades? What if there were an effortless way to accelerate the benefits of meditation?

> *The highest activities of consciousness have their origins in physical occurrences of the brain, just as the loveliest melodies are not too sublime to be expressed by notes.*
>
> — W. SOMERSET MAUGHAM

There is a way, and the technology exists. Based on decades of validated biofeedback research, brain wave training can help you experience the many benefits of meditation and optimize all aspects of cerebral performance. As Edward A. Taub, MD, explains, "You don't have to learn how to meditate; this technology literally meditates you."

Robert Cosgrove, MD, PhD, a biomedical engineer and expert in reversing the negative effects associated with age, notes, "Technologies altering brainwave patterns have great potential for promoting optimal cerebral performance, and long-term use may delay deterioration of the brain traditionally associated with aging."

In addition to preventing decline, brain wave training may also be helpful in improving intelligence throughout life. Siegfried Othmer, PhD, another pioneer in the field of biofeedback, reports that brain wave training can improve performance in reading comprehension, memory-related tasks, and logic-handling abilities. In one study of children with IQ scores below 100, Othmer found that brain wave training resulted in average gains of 23 IQ points. Furthermore, one year later, the subjects had maintained their gains as well as demonstrating significant improvements in self-concept, creativity, and concentration.

For many years, brain wave training involved going to a therapist's office, having electrodes applied to your scalp with a sticky paste, and sitting in front of a computer screen while you learned how to manipulate your brain waves into the ideal states for creativity, concentration, stress reduction, a good night's sleep, or meditation.

Biofeedback research has accelerated dramatically over the past thirty years. New technology makes brain wave training accessible to anyone with a pair of headphones and an audio player.

The Brain Sync Program

The *Brain Sync: Improve Your Mind as You Age* brain wave training audio program utilizes an audio technology that synchronizes and balances your brain for greater resilience, brilliance, and flexibility.

You can download your complimentary audio program at www.brainpowerdownload.com (coupon code: MeditateMe). A CD can also be purchased at the same website.

The audio program contains four tracks:

- Track 1 (*Introduction and Instructions for Listening*)
- Track 2 (*Pure Coherence*) refreshes your brain, clears mental fog, and focuses your mind like a laser beam. It also works as a natural antidepressant to boost your mood and energy levels. You'll feel alert and energized as your ability to think, concentrate, and store information is improved dramatically.
- Track 3 (*Deep Resonance*) allows you to effortlessly reach depths of meditation that would otherwise take years of practice to attain. As you listen, muscles relax, fears vanish, and stress fades; negative thoughts are washed away by streams of creative insight.
- Track 4 (*Slow-Wave Sleep*) encourages restful, re-generative sleep. With regular use of this track, you'll establish healthier sleep patterns and feel more refreshed in the morning.

All three main tracks facilitate the remarkable mental state known as hemispheric synchronization, which supports whole-brain thinking. Most people tend to favor one hemisphere over the other or shift between left-brain (analytical) and right-brain (imaginative) dominance in cycles that last from thirty minutes to three hours. While one hemisphere is dominant, the attributes and skills of the other are less available.

When both hemispheres operate in harmony, you enjoy a profound synergy of logic and imagination. Your mind becomes sharper, more focused, and more lucid. You synthesize and solve problems with greater speed. And you may be delighted to discover that you are more in touch with your emotions and intuition, and more receptive to creative insight.

How Brain Sync Works: The Training-Wheel Effect

Brain Sync harmonically layers pure and precisely tuned sound waves called "binaural beat frequencies" behind soothing musical tones to gently guide your brain into balance. A binaural beat frequency is an audio phenomenon that occurs in the brain when two slightly different sine waves are delivered to either ear through headphones. A sine wave is a continuous wave with a constant frequency and amplitude. For example, a sine wave of 100 Hz played in the left ear plus another one at 107 Hz in the right ear will produce a perception of a pulsating beat of 7 Hz. (*Hz* is the abbreviation for *hertz* — not the rental car company but the standard unit for measuring cycles per second.)

In other words, the two hemispheres of the brain function together to "hear" not the external sound signals but instead a third "phantom" beat, which is the mathematical difference between the two tones. The beat is not coming through the headphones but is perceived and experienced within the brain. It sounds like a soft, gentle drumbeat.

Discovered in 1839 by German physicist Heinrich Wilhelm Dove, binaural beats were just a curious anomaly until 1973, when Gerald Oster, MD, published his landmark article entitled "Auditory Beats in the Brain." Working at Mount Sinai Hospital in New York City, Dr. Oster found that binaural beats evoked change in the electrical activity of the listener's brain. This tendency for brain waves to resonate sympathetically is known as the frequency following response.

In the same way you might tap your foot to the rhythm of a song, brain activity naturally falls into rhythm with binaural beats. This frequency-following response means that binaural beats can be orchestrated to influence our brain waves, thus altering our states of consciousness. Different brain wave types are associated with different mental states, such as alpha for relaxation, beta for concentration, theta for meditation, and delta for sleep.

Michael Hutchison, author of *Megabrain: New Tools and Techniques for Brain Growth and Mind Expansion*, explains, "Research results show that parts of the brain, and eventually large areas of the brain, resonate sympathetically to this 'phantom' binaural beat, like a crystal goblet vibrates in response to a pure musical tone. Brain Sync audio programs thus provide a highly effective method for rapidly altering brain wave activity to boost you into specific, expanded states of consciousness." Hutchison describes the technology as "training wheels for your brain."

Catching the Perfect Wave

Brain waves — represented by squiggly lines on an electroencephalogram (EEG) monitor — show the speed at which neurons fire. Each time a neuron fires, an electromagnetic spark of energy is released, setting off a chain reaction among other neurons. The speed of the connection correlates to the speed of the frequency. For example, beta brain waves (associated with alertness) oscillate at much faster speeds than delta waves (associated with sleep).

You have your own unique brain wave patterns that function habitually. Some of these brain wave habits are useful, and others need some fine-tuning. When your brain is functioning efficiently, your brain waves are "in sync" with your activity, but stress or lack of sleep can interfere with this natural, harmonious relationship. Brain Sync technology can help you coordinate your brain waves with your desired behavior so that you can overcome stress, improve sleep, and enjoy the benefits of meditation, effortlessly. It can also support the development of new patterns that will improve your mind as you age.

Types of Brain Waves

In the 1930s, researchers began to identify several different types of brain waves that correspond to specific mental states.

Beta and Gamma Waves: The Key to Focus and Concentration

Beta and gamma waves (12–40 Hz) are correlated with the fastest of all the brain wave states — neurons fire rapidly and abundantly. These brain wave states are associated with alertness and focus. Beta is the best modality for activities where directed attention and high levels of concentration are needed. Biofeedback therapists often use beta training to treat attention deficit disorder (ADD).

Even if you don't have ADD, beta waves support mental alertness. They are beneficial for any activities that require focus and concentration. Beta waves help you prepare to take an exam, play sports, give a presentation, analyze and organize information, and perform other activities for which mental clarity is essential.

Some researchers refer to brain waves at the level of 40 Hz as gamma waves (others do not distinguish gamma waves as a distinct class but include them in beta waves). Nobel laureate Sir Francis Crick and other scientists believe that the 40 Hz frequency plays a special role in advanced cognition and high-level information processing.

Pure Coherence, track 2 on the Brain Sync audio program, features the 40 Hz frequency so that you can cultivate a sharper mind, greater clarity, and increased ability to concentrate.

Alpha Waves: The Gateway to Relaxation and Creativity

When you begin to relax, your brain activity slows from the rapid patterns of beta into the more gentle waves of alpha (7–12 Hz). In alpha, you experience a liberating sense of peace and well-being. "Subtle and ineffable" are the words used by pioneering biofeedback researcher Lester Fehmi, PhD, to describe the deep enjoyment of the alpha experience. Joe Kamiya, PhD, another leading researcher, posits that the pleasure associated with alpha may come from "letting go of anxieties."

Alpha is the gateway into deeper states of consciousness. When alpha brain waves become stronger, logical left-brain activity — which normally acts as a filter or censor to the subconscious — drops its guard. This allows the more intuitive, creative depths of the mind to become increasingly influential.

Deep Resonance, track 3 on the Brain Sync audio program, layers alpha with theta waves to promote deeply pleasurable states of relaxation.

Theta Waves: The Realm of Deep Insight and Meditation

Theta waves (4–7 Hz) are associated with the most elusive and extraordinary realm of consciousness. We normally experience theta fleetingly, upon awakening or drifting off to sleep. It allows access to the intuitive wisdom that resides just below the surface of normal waking consciousness.

Sudden flashes of insight — "Aha" and "Eureka" moments — are the province of the theta state. Theta inspires creativity, enhances learning and dream recall, reduces stress, and awakens extrasensory perception. At the very least, theta is a tranquil state of mind that brings many rejuvenating benefits.

Melinda Maxfield of the Foundation for Shamanic Studies notes that shamans from many cultures have found ways to access the theta state. One method, common to many indigenous cultures throughout history, is to use drumbeats struck in the theta range of 4.5 cycles per second.

Many great leaps of creative genius came in the theta state. Einstein's theory of relativity came to him in a daydream, as he envisioned himself surfing on a sunbeam into infinity. August Kekulé solved one of the most challenging problems in the history of organic chemistry — the conundrum of the structure of the benzene ring — when he fell into a reverie in his easy chair (there's some debate as to whether he was aided by a few glasses of fine brandy). In his mind's eye, Kekulé saw a vivid image of a snake chasing its own tail, an image that showed him the missing molecular puzzle piece. Archimedes's famous "Eureka" moment, when he intuited one of his principles of hydrostatics, came as he relaxed in the bath. Of course, these discoveries wouldn't have occurred without years of focused work and intention to set the stage, but the creative leaps, in which the pieces of the puzzle seem to effortlessly and vividly fall into place, are usually associated with the deeply relaxed, meditative theta state.

It normally takes considerable training to enter and maintain this state for longer periods of time. Advanced meditators learn to balance on the tightrope of theta, experiencing timeless states of reverie, vivid imagery, and access to insight and intuition.

Deep Resonance, track 3 on the Brain Sync audio program, layers theta with alpha waves so that you can experience the many benefits of meditation.

Delta Waves: The Palace of Sleep, Healing, and Regeneration

Long, slow, undulating delta waves (0–4 Hz) are the slowest of the four brain wave frequencies and are associated with sleep. Delta facilitates high-quality, restorative sleep, essential to healing and renewal.

Slow-Wave Sleep, track 4 on the Brain Sync audio program, offers a soothing pattern of delta waves hidden beneath the sound of ocean waves to help you sleep soundly.

Instructions for Listening

The best aspect of working with Brain Sync is that you don't have to do anything. You will experience tremendous benefits just by listening.

For best results, listen to only one track per session, as each one provides a unique experience. You may, however, listen to the different tracks at separate intervals throughout the day. And only listen with headphones — the stereo effect is essential to producing hemispheric synchronization. Here's the best way to listen to each of the three main tracks (tracks 2–4).

- Track 2 (*Pure Coherence*): Beta and gamma waves increase mental clarity and alertness, so start your day with the *Pure Coherence* track (it's not recommended for nighttime use). Boosting gamma wave activity will enhance all your senses and perception. Listen to this track before doing anything that requires your full attention. In addition to sharpening your concentration and focus, the frequencies on this track enhance hand-eye coordination. Golfers, tennis players, and other athletes find that listening just before competing helps them enter the state of "flow," also known as "relaxed concentration" or "the zone," which can enhance enjoyment and performance.

- Track 3 (*Deep Resonance*): Alpha and theta waves gently guide your mind into a relaxed, meditative state. Many people like to begin their day with meditation, finding that a dose of theta waves in the morning helps them maintain more ease and mindfulness. And since many people experience a dip in their energy later in the day, listening to the *Deep Resonance* track in the afternoon will refresh your mind and give you a second wind. Find a time that works best for you and experiment with regular practice.

- Track 4 (*Slow-Wave Sleep*): Hidden beneath the calming sound of ocean waves, delta frequencies ease your brain out of the rapid rhythms of beta into the deepest levels of sleep, known as slow-wave sleep. Slow-wave sleep plays a vital role in health and well-being. Deprivation of this sleep state can lead to unpleasant feelings of grogginess, depression, and general malaise. *Slow-Wave Sleep* is free of music and words, making it easier to drift off to a deep, refreshing sleep. Listen when you want to take a nap or before bed. If you wake up in the middle of the night and find it hard to go back to sleep, this track will gently lull you back to dreamland. You can set your audio player to automatically replay this track during the night. Even if your lifestyle doesn't allow for a full eight hours of sleep, a few hours of slow-wave sleep will help you wake feeling refreshed and revitalized.

Brain Sync Questions and Answers

Q. *Can I use Brain Sync as a substitute for meditation?*

A. It's best to think of Brain Sync as a complement or adjunct to meditation. Brain Sync will help you generate the same brain wave patterns as measured in advanced meditators. Meditation adepts find the program deepens their experience, and beginners find that using the program makes it much easier to develop and sustain a meditation practice. Patricia Joudry, coauthor of *Sound Therapy: Music to Recharge Your Brain*, says this about the Brain Sync program: "Listening was like having my brain lifted above my head and bathed in golden light. The mind-still and blissful peace that Brain Sync induced was comparable with the highest states of meditation that I have ever experienced."

Q. *Do I need any special equipment?*

A. All you need is a pair of headphones and an audio player. Any standard headphones work, including earbuds or noise-cancelling headphones; use whatever is most comfortable for you.

Q. *Why do I need to listen with headphones?*

A. The positive benefits of Brain Sync technology are predicated on the coordinated stereo effect — different frequencies played in each ear combine in the brain to produce specific brain waves.

Q. *Can I get the benefits of Brain Sync by listening on my iPod?*

A. Yes.

Q. *Is there anything I can do to enhance the experience of using Brain Sync?*

A. Find a comfortable position, either sitting or lying down with your spine straight. Close your eyes and breathe deeply as you let the waves wash through your brain.

Q. *Is Brain Sync safe?*

A. When used properly, Brain Sync is completely safe. These programs have been used successfully and safely by millions of people. Individuals with epilepsy or anyone who has been diagnosed with a neuroelectrical malfunction, such as being prone to seizures, shouldn't use Brain Sync without professional supervision.

Q. *Can children listen to Brain Sync?*

A. No. Brain wave training is not recommended for children under the age of twelve, unless under the supervision of a qualified biofeedback therapist.

Q. *Can I listen to the sound tracks while I do other things?*

A. You will get the greatest benefit if you listen in a comfortable position, without distraction, and with your eyes closed. Do not listen while driving or operating a machine.

Q. *How long will it take before I experience results?*

A. Most people feel the effects from the very first use. Moreover, brain wave training has a cumulative, positive effect. After a month or two, you'll realize that you've achieved benefits, such as greater clarity of thought, increased ability to cope with stress, and sharper memory.

Q. *Do I need to listen to the entire Brain Sync program every day?*

A. No. Each track is designed for specific results and benefits. You can listen to just one track or all of them, depending on your specific needs and goals.

Q. *Does Brain Sync require any sort of belief system?*

A. No. Brain Sync is based on a scientific understanding of brain waves and does not require any particular belief system to be effective.

Q. *Does Brain Sync support general healing and wellness?*

A. Sound sleep and meditation contribute to general health and wellness. And neurosurgeon Douglas Applewhite, MD, reports, "We tested Brain Sync on patients before, during, and after surgery. The programs seem to facilitate more rapid recovery. The comments from these patients were very positive in terms of relaxing and helping them manage the pain as well as aiding in their recovery."

Q. *Can you summarize the benefits of Brain Sync?*

A. Brain Sync facilitates greater coherence throughout your brain. Enhanced coherence is associated with improvements in creative thinking, intuitive aware-ness, accelerated learning, mindfulness, memory, and perceived well-being. The Brain Sync audio pro-gram is designed to liberate your brain power and improve your mind as you age.

CHAPTER NINE

Last Words

*B*rain Power: Improve Your Mind as You Age is based on the confluence of timeless wisdom, practical experience, and the latest research. Contemporary science has established that you can improve your mind as you age, and you can begin that process of improvement now.

Start by embracing a positive, optimistic, "counterclockwise" attitude toward aging. Find a guiding purpose for your life and focus on gratitude, forgiveness, and humor. Continuous learning is the true fountain of youth, so learn something new every day and embrace fresh challenges. Oxygenate your brain and sharpen your wits by creating an approach to exercise that you enjoy, and be mindful of the simple principles of healthy eating. Surround yourself with beauty and a positive, multisensory, stimulus-rich environment. Invest in your social wealth, and cultivate the practice of relaxation daily.

Imagine the wonderful new world that would emerge if a critical mass of people applied these simple principles. (And imagine the huge savings in health-care costs!) In the preface to *Brave New World*, Aldous Huxley advises that the best way to evaluate all things in life is to imagine that we are viewing them from the perspective of our final hours. And in *The Seven Habits of Highly Effective People*, Stephen Covey's second habit of effectiveness is "Begin with the End in Mind." The end of this book can serve as a catalyst for the beginning of an effective renaissance of your youthful vitality. Put these principles into practice so that when it's time to say your last words (and research suggests that if you apply what you've learned in this book, that time will come later rather than sooner), you can say something along the lines of our top ten favorite last words.

Top Ten Favorite Last Words

I think I'm beginning to learn something about art.

— PIERRE AUGUST RENOIR

Get my swan costume ready.

— ANNA PAVLOVA, ballerina

I should never have switched from Scotch to Martinis.

— HUMPHREY BOGART

Oh my, it is very beautiful over there.

— THOMAS EDISON

Oh wow. Oh wow. Oh wow.

— STEVE JOBS

Either that wallpaper goes, or I do.

— OSCAR WILDE,
while sipping champagne on his deathbed

Die, my dear? Why that's the last thing I'll do!

— GROUCHO MARX

And now for a final word from our sponsor.

— CHARLES GUSSMAN,
scriptwriter for many popular radio and TV shows

More light!

— JOHANN WOLFGANG VON GOETHE

I am about to — or I am going to — die:
either expression is correct.

— DOMINIQUE BOUHOURS,
French Jesuit, essayist, and grammarian

Age is opportunity no less,
Than youth itself, though in another dress,
And as the evening twilight fades away,
The sky is filled with stars, invisible by day.

— HENRY WADSWORTH LONGFELLOW

References

Introduction: A Whole New Brain

Page 1 *The brain is...the most complex thing*: James D. Watson, *Discovering the Brain* (Washington, DC: National Academy Press, 1992), iii.

Page 5 *Your brain is designed to improve*: Richard Restak, *Mozart's Brain and the Fighter Pilot: Unleashing Your Brain's Potential* (New York: Three Rivers Press, 2002), 41.

Page 5 *We can indeed form new brain cells*: Katie Hafner, "Exercise Your Brain, or Else You'll...Uh...," *New York Times*, May 3, 2008, www .nytimes.com/2008/05/03/technology/03brain.html.

Page 6 *The power of positive thinking*: Abigail Zuger, "The Brain: Malleable, Capable, Vulnerable," review of *The Brain That Changes Itself: Stories of Personal Triumph from the Frontiers of Brain Science*, by Norman Doidge, *New York Times*, May 29, 2007, www.nytimes.com/2007/05/29/health /29book.html.

Page 6 *Sir Charles Sherrington*: Charles Scott Sherrington, *Man on His Nature* (New York: Cambridge University Press, 2009), 237.

Page 7 *number of connections is "virtually infinite"*: Tony Buzan, *Use Both Sides of Your Brain*, 3rd ed. (New York: Plume, 1991), 10. See also P. K. Anokhin, Cybernetics of Functional Systems: Selected Works [in Russian] (Moscow: Meditsina, 1998).

Page 7 *The brain has an almost boundless*: Marco Iacoboni, personal communication with the authors, July 1, 2011.

Page 7 *If the human brain were so simple*: George Edgin Pugh, *The Biological Origin of Human Values* (London: Routledge, 1978), 154.

Page 9 *Mother Nature has plainly not entrusted*: Matt Ridley, *Genome: The Autobiography of a Species in 23 Chapters* (New York: HarperPerennial, 2000), 77.

Page 9 *I was exhilarated by the new realization*: Bruce H. Lipton, *The Biology of Belief: Unleashing the Power of Consciousness, Matter and Miracles* (Santa Rosa, CA: Elite Books, 2005), xv.

Chapter I: Think Counterclockwise

Page 12 *Langer's remarkable "counterclockwise" study*: Ellen J. Langer, *Counterclockwise: Mindful Health and the Power of Possibility* (New York: Ballantine Books, 2009).

Page 13 *Despite their obvious and extreme*: Ibid., 10.

Page 13 *Simply having a positive attitude*: Ibid., 23.

Page 14 *While exercise and eating well*: Ellen J. Langer, personal communication with the authors, October 26, 2010.

Page 14 *I have come to believe less*: Langer, *Counterclockwise*, 11.

Page 14 *Beginning in 1975, she surveyed*: Becca R. Levy et al., "Longevity Increased by Positive Self-Perceptions of Aging," *Journal of Personality and Social Psychology* 83, no. 2 (2002): 261–70.

Page 15 *Expectations determine outcomes*: Deepak Chopra and David Simon, *Grow Younger, Live Longer: 10 Steps to Reverse Aging* (New York: Harmony Books, 2001), 19.

Page 15 *So this doesn't seem like magic*: Valerie Gremillion, personal communication with the authors, June 17, 2011.

Page 16 *Learned Optimism*: Martin E. P. Seligman, *Learned Optimism: How to Change Your Mind and Your Life* (New York: Pocket Books, 1998).

Page 16 *The defining characteristic of pessimists*: Ibid., 4.

Page 18 *Neurons that fire together wire together*: Donald O. Hebb, *The Organization of Behavior: A Neuropsychological Theory* (London: Psychology Press, 2002), 213.

Page 19 *The Mind and the Brain*: Jeffrey M. Schwartz and Sharon Begley, *The Mind and the Brain: Neuroplasticity and the Power of Mental Force* (New York: ReganBooks, 2002).

Page 20 *Another method for mindfully changing*: Byron Katie, *Loving What Is: Four Questions That Can Change Your Life* (New York: Three Rivers Press, 2003).

Page 20 *An unquestioned mind is the world of suffering.*: Byron Katie on Twitter, January 14, 2011.

Page 21 *The greatest thing is to give thanks*: Albert Schweitzer, *Albert Schweitzer: Thoughts for Our Times*, ed. Erica Anderson (Mount Vernon, NY: Peter Pauper Press, 1975), 16.

Page 22 *In an experimental comparison*: "Gratitude and Well-Being," Emmons Lab, last modified February 17, 2011, http://psychology.ucdavis.edu/Labs/emmons/PWT/index.cfm?Section=4.

Page 23 *When Bad Things Happen to Good People*: Harold S. Kushner, *When Bad Things Happen to Good People* (New York: Anchor Books, 2004).

Page 23 *The practice of forgiveness boosts*: Fred Luskin, *Forgive for Good: A Proven Prescription for Health and Happiness* (San Francisco: HarperSanFrancisco, 2003).

Page 24 *Forgiving releases you from the punishment*: Doc Childre and Howard Martin, *The HeartMath Solution: The Institute of HeartMath's Revolutionary Program for Engaging the Power of the Heart's Intelligence* (San Francisco: HarperSanFrancisco, 2000), 123.

Page 26 *systematically replace every single thought*: Pierre Pradervand, *The Gentle Art of Blessing: A Simple Practice That Will Transform You and Your World* (New York: Atria, 2009), 13.

Page 26 *Anatomy of an Illness as Perceived by the Patient*: Norman Cousins,

Anatomy of an Illness as Perceived by the Patient: Reflections on Healing and Regeneration (New York: Norton, 2005), 43.

Page 27 *Journal of the American Medical Association*: Hajime Kimata, "Effect of Humor on Allergen-Induced Wheal Reactions," *Journal of the American Medical Association* 285, no. 6 (2001): 738, doi: 10.1001 /jama.285.6.738.

Page 27 *increases our heart rate*: "Fun Facts," *LaughLab*, accessed August 8, 2011, www.laughlab.co.uk.

Page 28 *smiling improves mood*: Chris L. Kleinke, Thomas R. Peterson, and Thomas R. Rutledge, "Effects of Self-Generated Facial Expressions on Mood," *Journal of Personality and Social Psychology* 74, no. 1 (1998): 272–79. See also Paul Ekman, *Emotions Revealed: Understanding Faces and Feelings* (New York: Henry Holt, 2003).

Page 29 *Becca Levy, PhD, exposed*: Becca Levy, "Improving Memory in Old Age through Implicit Self-Stereotyping," *Journal of Personality and Social Psychology* 71, no. 6 (1996): 1092–1107.

Page 29 *Negative stereotypes of aging*: Becca R. Levy et al., "Age Stereotypes Held Earlier in Life Predict Cardiovascular Events in Later Life," *Psychological Science* 20, no. 3 (2009): 296–98.

Page 29 *In other studies, Dr. Levy*: Becca R. Levy et al., "Reducing Cardiovascular Stress with Positive Self-Stereotypes of Aging," *Journal of Gerontology: Psychological Sciences* 55, no. 4 (2000): P205–13.

Page 30 *They also found that in cultures*: Becca Levy and Ellen Langer, "Aging Free from Negative Stereotypes: Successful Memory in China and among the American Deaf," *Journal of Personality and Social Psychology* 66, no. 6 (1994): 989–97.

Page 33 *The Image of the Elderly in Prime-Time*: George Gerbner, *Against the Mainstream: The Selected Works of George Gerbner*, ed. Michael Morgan (New York: Peter Lang, 2002).

Page 33 *Mass media, particularly television*: George Gerbner, "Learning Productive Aging as a Social Role: The Lessons of Television," in *Achieving a Productive Aging Society*, ed. Scott A. Bass, Francis G. Caro, and Yung-Ping Chen (Westport, CT: Auburn House, 1993), 207.

Page 33 *Negative stereotyping of the elderly*: Latika Vasil and Hannelore Wass,

"Portrayal of the Elderly in the Media: A Literature Review and Implications for Educational Gerontologists," *Educational Gerontology* 19, no. 1 (1993): 71–85.

Page 34 *goes out of its way to make aging*: Dave Barry, *Dave Barry Turns 40* (New York: Crown, 1990), 76, 84.

Page 34 *The Art of Aging*: Alice Matzkin and Richard Matzkin, *The Art of Aging: Celebrating the Authentic Aging Self* (Boulder, CO: Sentient, 2009).

Page 36 *deepest and richest work*: Raymond Keene, personal communication with the authors, July 29, 2011.

Page 43 *Patricia A. Boyle, PhD, of Rush University Medical Center*: P.A. Boyle et al., "Effect of a Purpose in Life on Risk of Incident Alzheimer Disease and Mild Cognitive Impairment in Community-Dwelling Older Persons," *Archives General Psychiatry* 67, no. 3 (2010): 304–10.

Chapter 2: Be a Lifelong Learner

Page 46 *No matter how old you may be*: Richard Restak, *Mozart's Brain and the Fighter Pilot: Unleashing Your Brain's Potential* (New York: Three Rivers Press, 2002), 41.

Page 47 *Stimulating the brain makes it grow*: Norman Doidge, *The Brain That Changes Itself: Stories of Personal Triumph from the Frontiers of Brain Science* (New York: Penguin, 2007), 43.

Page 47 *change hundreds of millions*: Michael Merzenich et al., "Some Neurological Principles Relevant to the Origins of — and the Cortical Plasticity-Based Remediation of — Language Learning Impairments," in *Neuronal Plasticity: Building a Bridge from the Laboratory to the Clinic*, ed. Jordan Grafman and Yves Christen (New York: Springer, 1999), 169–87.

Page 48 *observed that rats who ran*: Marian Diamond and Janet Hopson, *Magic Trees of the Mind: How to Nurture Your Child's Intelligence, Creativity, and Healthy Emotions from Birth through Adolescence* (New York: Plume, 1999), 35.

Page 48 *Spending just 15 minutes a day*: Daniel G. Amen, ed., *Amen Brain Health Report*, April 2009, 1.

Page 48 *You can improve your mind*: Marco Iacoboni, personal communication with the authors, June 18, 2011.

Page 49 *The Magical Number Seven*: George A. Miller, "The Magical Number Seven, Plus or Minus Two: Some Limits on Our Capacity for Processing Information," *Psychological Review* 63, no. 2 (1956): 81–97.

Page 51 *The memorization and recitation*: Michael Knox Beran, "In Defense of Memorization," *City Journal*, Summer 2004, www.city-journal.org /html/14_3_defense_memorization.html.

Page 52 *Current Directions in Psychological Science*: Helga Noice and Tony Noice, "What Studies of Actors and Acting Can Tell Us about Memory and Cognitive Functioning," *Current Directions in Psychological Science* 15, no. 1 (2006): 14–18.

Page 56 *Master Your Memory*: Tony Buzan, *Master Your Memory* (London: BBC Books, 1998).

Page 56 *Buzan also pioneered*: Tony Buzan, *The Mind Map Book* (New York: Dutton, 1994).

Page 56 *Research has demonstrated*: "Why Mind Mapping Works — the Proof Is Here!," ThinkBuzan, accessed July 10, 2011, www.thinkbuzan.com /uk/articles/mindmappingworks.

Page 57 *Another great tool*: "Brain Fitness Program," Posit Science, accessed July 10, 2011, www.positscience.com/our-products/brain-fitness -program.

Page 57 *The program utilizes visual*: "How Does the Training Work?," Posit Science, accessed July 10, 2011, www.positscience.com/science /how-training-works/brain-training-works.

Page 57 *Proceedings of the National Academy*: Henry W. Mahncke et al., "Memory Enhancement in Healthy Older Adults Using a Brain Plasticity–Based Training Program: A Randomized, Controlled Study," *Proceedings of the National Academy of Sciences of the United States of America* 103, no. 33 (2006): 12523.

Page 57 *New England Journal of Medicine*: Joe Verghese et al., "Leisure Activities and the Risk of Dementia in the Elderly," *New England Journal of Medicine* 348, no. 25 (2003): 2508–16.

Page 58 *If you exercise and build up*: Joe Verghese in an interview (November

22, 2003) with Amanda Gardner, *HealthDay News*, "The Use-It-or-Lose-It Defense."

Page 58 *The infinite possibilities*: Raymond Keene, personal communication with the authors, July 31, 2011.

Page 59 *Music Making and Wellness Project*: Midori Koga, "The Music Making and Wellness Project," *American Music Teacher*, October/November 2001, 18–22.

Page 60 *You don't have to master it*: "Learning a Foreign Language Can Help You Live Longer," ABCNEWS.com, October 23, 2005, http://abc news.go.com/GMA/LivingLonger/story?id=1241571. See also Andrew Weil, *Healthy Aging: A Lifelong Guide to Your Physical and Spiritual Well-Being* (New York: Knopf, 2005).

Page 60 *Studies comparing the rate*: Mary J. Schleppegrell, "The Older Language Learner," September 1987, ERIC Clearinghouse on Languages and Linguistics (ED287313).

Page 61 *We've eliminated the traditional*: "Our Approach," Rosetta Stone, accessed July 11, 2011, http://secure.rosettastone.com/personal /how-it-works/our-approach.

Page 62 *Psychology and Aging*: Ellen Bialystok et al., "Bilingualism, Aging, and Cognitive Control: Evidence from the Simon Task," *Psychology and Aging* 19, no. 2 (2004): 290–303.

Page 63 *Johnson O'Connor conducted*: Johnson O'Connor, *English Vocabulary Builder* (Boston: Human Engineering Laboratory, 1948).

Page 63 *Juggling 'Can Boost Brain Power'*: "Juggling 'Can Boost Brain Power,'" BBC News, January 22, 2004, http://news.bbc.co.uk/2/hi /health/3417045.stm.

Page 63 *Juggling Good for the Brain*: "Juggling Good for the Brain, Study Shows," CNN.com, January 22, 2004, www.cnn.com/2004 /HEALTH/01/22/offbeat.juggling.brain.reut/.

Page 63 *Juggling Makes Your Brain Bigger*: Christian Nordqvist, "Juggling Makes Your Brain Bigger — New Study," *Medical News Today*, February 1, 2004, www.medicalnewstoday.com/releases/5615.php.

Page 63 *Neuroplasticity: Changes in Grey Matter*: Bogdan Draganski et al.,

"Neuroplasticity: Changes in Grey Matter Induced by Training," *Nature*, January 22, 2004, 311–12.

Page 65 *Another study, published in 2006*: Claudia Voelcker-Rehage and Klaus Willimczik, "Motor Plasticity in a Juggling Task in Older Adults — a Developmental Study," *Age and Ageing* 35, no. 4 (2006): 422–27.

Page 66 *New learning actually causes*: Amen, *Brain Health Report*, 1.

Page 66 *Lifelong learning and continued education*: Paul B. Baltes and Ursula M. Staudinger, "Wisdom: A Metaheuristic (Pragmatic) to Orchestrate Mind and Virtue toward Excellence," *American Psychologist* 55, no. 1 (2000): 122–36.

Page 67 *Wisdom has a profoundly positive*: Monika Ardelt, "Wisdom and Life Satisfaction in Old Age," *Journal of Gerontology: Psychological Sciences* 52B, no. 1 (1997): P15–27.

Page 67 *an expert knowledge system*: Baltes and Staudinger, "Wisdom."

Page 67 *How We Age*: Marc E. Agronin, *How We Age: A Doctor's Journey into the Heart of Growing Old* (Cambridge, MA: Da Capo Press, 2011), 12.

Chapter 3: Exercise for More Brain Power

Page 69 *The Roadmap to 100*: Walter M. Bortz and Randall Stickrod, *The Roadmap to 100: The Breakthrough Science of Living a Long and Healthy Life* (New York: Palgrave Macmillan, 2010).

Page 69 *Living Longer for Dummies*: Walter M. Bortz, *Living Longer for Dummies* (Hoboken, NJ: Wiley, 2001).

Page 69 *Almost everything we have been*: Walter M. Bortz II's website, accessed August 9, 2011, http://walterbortz.com.

Page 70 *Exercise provides a 30-year*: Bortz, *Living Longer for Dummies*, 45.

Page 70 *Meditations on First Philosophy*: René Descartes, *Meditations on First Philosophy: In Which the Existence of God and the Distinction of the Soul from the Body Are Demonstrated*, 3rd ed., trans. Donald A. Cress (Indianapolis: Hackett, 1993).

Page 71 *Brain Rules*: John Medina, *Brain Rules: 12 Principles for Surviving and Thriving at Work, Home, and School* (Seattle: Pear Press, 2008).

Page 71 *Exercise zaps harmful*: John Medina, *Brain Rules* website, accessed August 9, 2011, www.brainrules.net/exercise.

Page 71 *It cuts risk of dementia*: Medina, *Brain Rules: 12 Principles*, 16.

Page 71 *one of the best treatments*: John J. Ratey, *Spark: The Revolutionary New Science of Exercise and the Brain* (New York: Little, Brown, 2008), 7.

Page 72 *unleashes a cascade*: Ibid., 4, 5.

Page 72 *In a fascinating experiment*: Peter Russell, *The Brain Book: Know Your Own Mind and How to Use It* (London: Routledge, 1994).

Page 75 *Aerobics was published*: Kenneth H. Cooper, *Aerobics* (New York: M. Evans, 1968).

Page 76 *Thirty minutes of aerobic activity*: Krista A. Barbour and James A. Blumenthal, "Exercise Training and Depression in Older Adults," *Neurobiology of Aging* 26, no. 1, supplement 1 (2005): 119–23.

Page 76 *aerobic exercise may not only*: "Staying Sharp," DukeHealth.org, last modified May 6, 2010, www.dukehealth.org/health_library/health _articles/staying_sharp.

Page 76 *Walking also sharpens memory*: Schaefer, S., et.al., (2010). "Cognitive performance is improved while walking: Differences in cognitive-sensorimotor couplings between children and young adults." *European Journal of Developmental Psychology* 7, no. 3, 371–89.

Page 77 *In a classic study, Fred H. Gage*: Gerd Kempermann, H. Georg Kuhn, and Fred H. Gage, "More Hippocampal Neurons in Adult Mice Living in an Enriched Environment," *Nature*, April 3, 1997, 493–95.

Page 78 *A study led by Steven N. Blair*: Nancy L. Chase, Xuemei Sui, and Steven N. Blair, "Swimming and All-Cause Mortality Risk Compared with Running, Walking, and Sedentary Habits in Men," *International Journal of Aquatic Research and Education* 2, no. 3 (2008): 213–23.

Page 78 *a study of more than forty thousand*: "New Study Reveals Swimming Can Cut Men's Risk of Dying in Half," *Medical News Today*, February 3, 2009, www.medicalnewstoday.com/releases/137549.php.

Page 79 *Izumi Tabata, PhD*: Izumi Tabata et al., "Effects of Moderate-Intensity Endurance and High-Intensity Intermittent Training on Anaerobic Capacity and VO2max," *Medicine and Science in Sports and Exercise* 28, no. 10 (1996): 1327–30.

Page 79 *Al Sears, MD, originator*: Al Sears, *PACE: The 12-Minute Fitness Revolution* (Royal Palm Beach, FL: Wellness Research Foundation, 2010).

Page 80 *A high-intensity, progressive*: Maria A. Fiatarone et al., "Exercise Training and Nutritional Supplementation for Physical Frailty in Very Elderly People," *New England Journal of Medicine* 330, no. 25 (1994): 1769–75.

Page 80 *other studies confirm*: Jennifer E. Layne and Miriam E. Nelson, "The Effects of Progressive Resistance Training on Bone Density: A Review," *Medicine and Science in Sports and Exercise* 31, no. 1 (1999): 25–30.

Page 80 *Strength Training Anatomy*: Frédéric Delavier, *Strength Training Anatomy*, 3rd ed. (Champaign, IL: Human Kinetics, 2010).

Page 81 *Nature designed your body*: Sears, *PACE*, 68.

Page 83 *Dean Ornish, MD, founder*: Dean Ornish, *The Spectrum: A Scientifically Proven Program to Feel Better, Live Longer, Lose Weight, and Gain Health* (New York: Ballantine Books, 2008).

Page 83 *The Pocket Idiot's Guide*: Ami Jayaprada Hirschstein, *The Pocket Idiot's Guide to 108 Yoga Poses* (New York: Alpha Books, 2006).

Page 83 *Stretching Anatomy*: Arnold G. Nelson and Jouko Kokkonen, *Stretching Anatomy* (Champaign, IL: Human Kinetics, 2007).

Page 83 *Framework by Nicholas A. DiNubile*: Nicholas A. DiNubile, *Framework: Your 7-Step Program for Healthy Muscles, Bones, and Joints* (Emmaus, PA: Rodale, 2005).

Page 85 *People in the cars think I'm crazy*: Marian Cleeves Diamond, interviewed in *Aging Today*, May/June 1998, a publication of the American Society on Aging.

Page 85 *The Great Balance and Stability Handbook*: Andre Noel Potvin and Chad Benson, *The Great Balance and Stability Handbook: The Quick Reference Guide to Balance and Stability Exercises* (Bellingham, WA: Productive Fitness Products, 2003).

Page 88 *British Medical Journal*: Paul Little et al., "Randomised Controlled Trial of Alexander Technique Lessons, Exercise, and Massage

(ATEAM) for Chronic and Recurrent Back Pain," *British Medical Journal*, August 19, 2008, www.bmj.com/content/337/bmj.a884.full.

Page 89 *A growing body*: "The Health Benefits of Tai Chi," *Harvard Women's Health Watch*, May 2009, www.health.harvard.edu/newsletters/Harvard _Womens_Health_Watch/2009/May/The-health-benefits-of-tai-chi.

Page 89 *Tai chi strengthens both*: Ibid.

Page 89 *Steven L. Wolf, PhD*: "Tai Chi for Older People Reduces Falls, May Help Maintain Strength," National Institute on Aging, May 2, 1996, www.nia.nih.gov/NewsAndEvents/PressReleases/PR19960502 TaiChi.htm.

Chapter 4: Mind Your Diet to Nourish Your Mind

Page 92 *If you want to have a great*: Daniel G. Amen, ed., *Amen Brain Health Report*, May 2009, 1.

Page 93 *Considering that your brain*: Ibid.

Page 94 *Your Body's Many Cries for Water*: F. Batmanghelidj, *Your Body's Many Cries for Water: You Are Not Sick, You Are Thirsty! Don't Treat Thirst with Medications!* (Vienna, VA: Global Health Solutions, 2008).

Page 94 *U.S. National Weight Control Registry*: Holly R. Wyatt et al., "Long-Term Weight Loss and Breakfast in Subjects in the National Weight Control Registry," *Obesity Research* 10, no. 2 (2002): 78–82.

Page 95 *researchers from the University of Toronto*: Randall J. Kaplan et al., "Dietary Protein, Carbohydrate, and Fat Enhance Memory Performance in the Healthy Elderly," *American Journal of Clinical Nutrition* 74, no. 5 (2001): 687–93. See also John E. Morley, "Food for Thought," *American Journal of Clinical Nutrition* 74, no. 5 (2001): 567–68.

Page 95 *children who ate breakfast*: David Benton and Megan Jarvis, "The Role of Breakfast and a Mid-morning Snack on the Ability of Children to Concentrate at School," *Physiology and Behavior* 90, no. 2–3 (2007): 382–85. See also David Benton, Alys Maconie, and Claire Williams, "The Influence of the Glycaemic Load of Breakfast on the Behaviour of Children in School," *Physiology and Behavior* 92, no. 4 (2007): 717–24; and C.-J. Huang et al., "Associations of Breakfast Skipping with Obesity and Health-Related Quality of Life: Evidence from a National

Survey in Taiwan," *International Journal of Obesity* 34, no. 4 (2010): 720–25.

Page 95 *Breakfast establishes the core support* : Valerie Gremillion, Personal communication with the authors, August 21, 2011.

Page 96 *a rating scale for the antioxidant*: U.S. Department of Agriculture, Agricultural Research Service, *USDA Database for the Oxygen Radical Absorbance Capacity (ORAC) of Selected Foods, Release 2* (Beltsville, MD: U.S. Department of Agriculture, Agricultural Research Service, 2010). See also ORACValues.com, accessed August 9, 2011, http:// oracvalues.com.

Page 97 *A review, by Gladys Block, PhD*: Gladys Block, Blossom Patterson, and Amy Subar, "Fruit, Vegetables, and Cancer Prevention: A Review of the Epidemiological Evidence," *Nutrition and Cancer* 18, no. 1 (1992): 1–29.

Page 98 *Current scientific evidence*: Satya S. Jonnalagadda et al., "Putting the Whole Grain Puzzle Together: Health Benefits Associated with Whole Grains — Summary of American Society for Nutrition 2010 Satellite Symposium," *Journal of Nutrition* 141, no. 5 (2011): 1011S–22S.

Page 99 *Americans consume an average*: Nancy Appleton and G. N. Jacobs, *Suicide by Sugar: A Startling Look at Our #1 National Addiction* (Garden City Park, NY: Square One, 2009).

Page 100 *Glucose (sugar) binds*: Tereza Hubkova, personal communication with the authors, June 29, 2011.

Page 101 *Carbohydrates, and especially*: Cynthia Kenyon, personal communication with the authors, June 3, 2011.

Page 102 *[They] interfere with the metabolism*: Deborah Gleason, "Frankenfats," Doctor Deb Natural Health, accessed July 12, 2011, www .doctordebnaturalhealth.com/frankenfats.html.

Page 102 *There is no safe amount*: Institute of Medicine of the National Academies, Food and Nutrition Board, *Dietary Reference Intakes for Energy, Carbohydrate, Fiber, Fat, Fatty Acids, Cholesterol, Protein, and Amino Acids* (Washington, DC: National Academies Press, 2005), 504.

Page 103 *Extensive research shows*: University of Granada, "Consuming Extra Virgin Olive Oil Helps to Combat Degenerative Diseases Such as

Cancer, Study Suggests," *ScienceDaily*, January 21, 2008, www.science daily.com/releases/2008/01/080117101503.htm.

Page 104 *low-glycemic meals are more satisfying*: Hyla Cass, MD, personal communication with the authors, August 15, 2011.

Page 104 *Although it's very useful*: Hyla Cass and Patrick Holford, *Natural Highs: Supplements, Nutrition, and Mind-Body Techniques to Help You Feel Good All the Time* (New York: Avery, 2002), 31.

Page 106 *My patients are often amazed*: Amen, *Brain Health Report*, 7.

Page 106 *The right nutrients in the proper amounts*: Michael F. Roizen, *Real-Age: Are You as Young as You Can Be?* (New York: William Morrow, 1999), 141.

Page 107 *The evidence suggests that people*: Godfrey P. Oakley Jr., "Eat Right *and* Take a Multivitamin," *New England Journal of Medicine* 338, no. 15 (1998): 1060–61.

Page 107 *in the medical journal the Lancet*: David Benton and Gwilym Roberts, "Effect of Vitamin and Mineral Supplementation on Intelligence of a Sample of Schoolchildren," *Lancet* 331, no. 8578 (1988): 140–43.

Page 107 *eat wild, fresh, organic*: Mark Hyman, *The UltraMind Solution: Fix Your Broken Brain by Healing Your Body First; The Simple Way to Defeat Depression, Overcome Anxiety and Sharpen Your Mind* (New York: Scribner, 2010), 114.

Page 108 *Vitamin C and the Common Cold*: Linus Pauling, *Vitamin C and the Common Cold* (San Francisco: Freeman, 1970).

Page 108 *Seminars in Preventive and Alternative*: Mark A. Moyad and Maile A. Combs, "Vitamin C Dietary Supplements: An Objective Review of the Clinical Evidence — Part I," *Seminars in Preventive and Alternative Medicine* 3, no. 1 (2007): 25–35.

Page 108 *The more we study vitamin C*: Kathleen M. Zelman, "The Benefits of Vitamin C: What Can Vitamin C Do for Your Health?," WebMD, accessed August 2, 2011, www.webmd.com/diet/guide/the-benefits-of -vitamin-c.

Page 110 *effective in treating and possibly preventing*: "Probiotics: Bacteria That Offer Health Benefits," Mayo Clinic, June 8, 2009, www.mayo clinic.org/news2009-mchi/5340.html.

Page 110 *Researchers from Ohio State University*: Wei Zhang et al., "Probiotic *Lactobacillus acidophilus* Enhances the Immunogenicity of an Oral Rotavirus Vaccine in Gnotobiotic Pigs," *Vaccine* 26, no. 29–30 (2008): 3655–61.

Page 110 *a Swedish study suggests*: "*Lactobacillus reuteri* Good for Health, Swedish Study Finds," *ScienceDaily*, November 4, 2010, www.science daily.com/releases/2010/11/101102131302.htm.

Page 111 *American Journal of Epidemiology*: Tze-Pin Ng et al., "Curry Consumption and Cognitive Function in the Elderly," *American Journal of Epidemiology* 164, no. 9 (2006): 898–906.

Page 111 *might be one of the most promising*: Tsuyoshi Hamaguchi, Kenjiro Ono, and Masahito Yamada, "Curcumin and Alzheimer's Disease," *CNS Neuroscience and Therapeutics* 16, no. 5 (2010): 285–97, doi: 10.1111/j.1755-5949.2010.00147.x.

Page 111 *an important contributor*: Mariano Malaguarnera et al., "L-Carnitine Treatment Reduces Severity of Physical and Mental Fatigue and Increases Cognitive Functions in Centenarians: A Randomized and Controlled Clinical Trial," *American Journal of Clinical Nutrition* 86, no. 6 (2007): 1738–44.

Page 112 *Supplement Your Prescription*: Hyla Cass, *Supplement Your Prescription: What Your Doctor Doesn't Know about Nutrition* (Laguna Beach, CA: Basic Health, 2007).

Page 112 *The prescription drugs*: Hyla Cass, MD, personal communication with the authors, August 15, 2011.

Page 112 *The truth is, most doctors*: Hyla Cass, MD, personal communication with the authors, August 15, 2011.

Page 113 *Journal of Alzheimer's Disease*: Marjo H. Eskelinen et al., "Midlife Coffee and Tea Drinking and the Risk of Late-Life Dementia: A Population-Based CAIDE Study," *Journal of Alzheimer's Disease* 16, no. 1 (2009): 85–91.

Page 113 *a report in the European Journal*: B. M. van Gelder et al., "Coffee Consumption Is Inversely Associated with Cognitive Decline in Elderly European Men: The FINE Study," *European Journal of Clinical Nutrition*

(2007) 61: 226–232. doi: 10.1038/sj.ejcn.1602495; published online 16 August 2006.

Page 114 *health effects of regular, moderate*: Stephen O'Grady, "Keep Cancer at Bay with a Cup of Coffee," Griffith University, June 15, 2011, www3 .griffith.edu.au/03/ertiki/tiki-read_article.php?articleId=30765.

Page 114 *In a presentation to the American Chemical Society*: Joe Vinson quoted in an article by Sophie L. Wilkinson, "Take Two Cups of Coffee and Call Me Tomorrow: Coffee and Chocolate Contain Antioxidants That May Promote Health," *Chemical Engineering News* 77, no. 15 (1999): 47–50.

Page 114 *Overall, the research shows*: Tomas DePaulis, "Wake Up and Smell the Research," *Science*, March 5, 1999, 1445.

Page 115 *Eating dark chocolate can raise*: "Boosting Brain Power — with Chocolate," *ScienceDaily*, February 22, 2007, www.sciencedaily.com /releases/2007/02/070221101326.htm.

Page 115 *The large body of evidence*: Eric L. Ding et al., "Chocolate and Prevention of Cardiovascular Disease: A Systematic Review," *Nutrition and Metabolism* 3, article 2 (2006), doi: 10.1186/1743-7075-3-2.

Page 115 *Stockholm Heart Epidemiology Program*: Janszky et al., "Chocolate Consumption and Mortality Following a First Acute Myocardial Infarction: The Stockholm Heart Epidemiology Program," *Journal of Internal Medicine* 266, no. 3 (2009): 248–57.

Page 116 *Moderate wine consumption*: "The Healing Power of Wine," *Wine Spectator*, May 31, 2009.

Page 117 *So the question is no longer*: Ibid. See also Eha Nurk et al., "Intake of Flavonoid-Rich Wine, Tea, and Chocolate by Elderly Men and Women Is Associated with Better Cognitive Test Performance," *Journal of Nutrition* 139, no. 1 (2009): 120–27.

Page 118 *YOU: Staying Young*: Michael F. Roizen and Mehmet C. Oz, *YOU: Staying Young; The Owner's Manual for Extending Your Warranty* (New York: Free Press, 2007).

Page 118 *Their answer: daily flossing*: "You: Staying Young: The Owner's Manual for Extending Your Warranty," Amazon.com, accessed August

15, 2011, www.amazon.com/You-Staying-Owners-Extending-Warranty
/dp/0743292561.

Page 119 *The attempt to cut calories*: Janet A. Tomiyama et al., "Low-Calorie
Dieting Increases Cortisol," *Psychosomatic Medicine* 72, no. 4 (2010):
357–64.

Page 120 *By eating foods of higher*: Steven Reinberg, "Low-Cal Diets May
Make You *Gain* Weight," Bloomberg Businessweek, April 8, 2010,
www.businessweek.com/lifestyle/content/healthday/637842.html. See
also David L. Katz, *Dr. David Katz's Flavor-Full Diet: Use Your Taste
Buds to Lose Pounds and Inches with This Scientifically Proven Plan* (Emmaus, PA: Rodale, 2007).

Page 121 *A study by researchers*: O. B. Pederson, "Enterotypes of the Human
Gut Microbiome," *Nature*, April 20, 2011, doi: 10.1038/nature09944.

Chapter 5: Create a Brain-Enhancing Environment

Page 124 *When you are optimistic*: "Alice Therapy: The Inspiring Alice Herz-
Sommer — Dancing under the Gallows," *Art Therapy* (blog), November 8, 2010, www.arttherapyblog.com/videos/alice-herz-sommer
-dancing-under-the-gallows/.

Page 125 *Throughout life, not just*: Richard Restak, *Mozart's Brain and the
Fighter Pilot: Unleashing Your Brain's Potential* (New York: Three
Rivers Press, 2002), 41.

Page 125 *In his classic experiments, Rosenzweig*: Mark R. Rosenzweig et al.,
"Effects of Environmental Complexity and Training on Brain Chemistry and Anatomy: A Replication and Extension," *Journal of Comparative
and Physiological Psychology* 55, no. 4 (1962): 429–37.

Page 125 *For each species there exists*: David Krech, Mark R. Rosenzweig,
and Edward L. Bennett, "Effects of Environmental Complexity and
Training on Brain Chemistry," *Journal of Comparative and Physiological
Psychology* 53, no. 6 (1960): 509–19.

Page 126 *Noise pollution adversely affects*: "Noise Pollution," U.S. Environmental Protection Agency, last modified July 7, 2011, www.epa.gov
/air/noise.html.

Page 127 *a paper in the journal Nature*: Frances H. Rauscher, Gordon L.

Shaw, and Katherine N. Ky, "Music and Spatial Task Performance," *Nature*, October 14, 1993, 611.

Page 127 *In a 2004 article, New Scientist*: Emily Singer, "Molecular Basis for Mozart Effect Revealed," *New Scientist*, April 23, 2004, www.new scientist.com/article/dn4918-molecular-basis-for-mozart-effect -revealed.html.

Page 129 *Health and Light*: John N. Ott, *Health and Light: The Extraordinary Study That Shows How Light Affects Your Health and Emotional Well-Being* (York, UK: Ariel Press, 2000).

Page 130 *in the journal Psychological Science*: Marc G. Berman, John Jonides, and Stephen Kaplan, "The Cognitive Benefits of Interacting with Nature," *Psychological Science* 19, no. 12 (2008): 1207–12.

Page 130 *In their book Earthing*: Clinton Ober, Stephen T. Sinatra, and Martin Zucker, *Earthing: The Most Important Health Discovery Ever?* (Laguna Beach, CA: Basic Health, 2010).

Page 132 *Aromatherapy in Dementia*: Clive Holmes and Clive Ballard, "Aromatherapy in Dementia," *Advances in Psychiatric Treatment* 10, no. 4 (2004): 296–300.

Page 132 *Nothing is more memorable*: Diane Ackerman, *A Natural History of the Senses* (New York: Vintage Books, 1991), 5.

Page 133 *The artist is intuitively*: Candace Jackson, "How Art Affects the Brain," *Wall Street Journal*, January 22, 2010, http://online.wsj.com /article/SB10001424052748703699204575017050699693576.html.

Page 134 *It doesn't take money*: Marian Diamond and Janet Hopson, *Magic Trees of the Mind: How to Nurture Your Child's Intelligence, Creativity, and Healthy Emotions from Birth through Adolescence* (New York: Plume, 1999), 9.

Page 134 *In his book Brain Rules*: John Medina, *Brain Rules: 12 Principles for Surviving and Thriving at Work, Home, and School* (Seattle: Pear Press, 2008).

Chapter 6: Cultivate Healthy Relationships (and Stay Sexy!)

Page 136 *American Journal of Public Health*: Valerie C. Crooks et al., "Social Network, Cognitive Function, and Dementia Incidence among Elderly Women," *American Journal of Public Health* 98, no. 7 (2008): 1221–27.

Page 136 *Whenever we have even*: Kathleen Doheny, "Staying Social May Keep Dementia at Bay," ABCNEWS.com, June 28, 2008, http://abc news.go.com/Health/Healthday/story?id=5262232.

Page 137 *Researchers from the Rush University*: Robert S. Wilson et al., "Loneliness and Risk of Alzheimer Disease," *Archives of General Psychiatry* 64, no. 2 (2007): 234–40.

Page 137 *David Spiegel, MD*: David Spiegel et al., "Effect of Psychosocial Treatment on Survival of Patients with Metastatic Breast Cancer," *Lancet* 334, no. 8668 (1989): 888–91.

Page 138 *American Sociological Review*: Miller McPherson, Lynn Smith-Lovin, and Matthew E. Brashears, "Social Isolation in America: Changes in Core Discussion Networks over Two Decades," *American Sociological Review* 71, no. 3 (2006): 353–75.

Page 138 *the groundbreaking book Loneliness*: John T. Cacioppo and William Patrick, *Loneliness: Human Nature and the Need for Social Connection* (New York: Norton, 2008), 108.

Page 139 *concluded that having close*: Raymond Keene, personal communication with the authors, August 1, 2011.

Page 140 *Sharing a meal with others daily*: Dan Buettner, *The Blue Zones: Lessons for Living Longer from the People Who've Lived the Longest* (Washington, DC: National Geographic, 2008).

Page 140 *the mentoring experiences allow*: Elizabeth Larkin, Sheila E. Sadler, and Joy Mahler, "Benefits of Volunteering for Older Adults Mentoring At-Risk Youth," *Journal of Gerontological Social Work* 44, no. 3–4 (2005): 23–37.

Page 141 *Warwick Anderson discovered*: "Does Pet Ownership Reduce Your Risk for Heart Disease?," *InterActions* 10, no. 3 (1992): 12–13.

Page 141 *the known effects of other*: James Serpell, *In the Company of Animals: A Study of Human-Animal Relationships* (Cambridge: Cambridge University Press, 1996), 101.

Page 142 *I have found that a key factor*: Eva Selhub, personal communication with the authors, May 19, 2011.

Page 143 *Frequency of sexual activity*: Stacy Tessler Lindau and Natalia Gavrilova, "Sex, Health, and Years of Sexually Active Life Gained Due to Good Health: Evidence from Two US Population Based Cross

Sectional Surveys of Ageing," *British Medical Journal* 340, article c810 (2010), doi: 10.1136/bmj.c810.

Page 143 *Sex can extend your life*: Walter M. Bortz, *Living Longer for Dummies* (Hoboken, NJ: Wiley, 2001), 125, 143.

Page 146 *Sex for One*: Betty Dodson, *Sex for One: The Joy of Selfloving* (New York: Three Rivers Press, 1996).

Page 146 *Exercise frequency*: Tina M. Penhollow and Michael Young, "Sexual Desirability and Sexual Performance: Does Exercise and Fitness Really Matter?," *Electronic Journal of Human Sexuality*, October 5, 2004, www .ejhs.org/volume7/fitness.html.

Page 147 *being able to be fully*: Peggy J. Kleinplatz et al., "The Components of Optimal Sexuality: A Portrait of 'Great Sex,'" *Canadian Journal of Human Sexuality* 18, no. 1–2 (2009): 1–13.

Page 148 *There are three possible*: Judith Martin, *Miss Manners' Guide to Excruciatingly Correct Behavior* (New York: Norton, 2005).

Page 149 *to be emotionally naked*: Kleinplatz et al., "Components of Optimal Sexuality."

Page 149 *Men over fifty, sixty*: Katherine Anne Forsythe, "Why I'd Rather Sleep with an Old Guy," Get a Second Wind, January 5, 2009, http://getasecondwind.com/content/articles/why-id-rather-sleep -with-an-old-guy/.

Chapter 7: Rest Peacefully to Delay Resting in Peace

Page 152 *Sleep is as critical*: Walter M. Bortz, *Living Longer for Dummies* (Hoboken, NJ: Wiley, 2001), 69.

Page 152 *The fundamental purpose*: Robert Stickgold, "The Simplest Way to Reboot Your Brain," *Harvard Business Review*, October 2009.

Page 155 *Edlund discovered*: Matthew Edlund, *The Power of Rest: Why Sleep Alone Is Not Enough; A 30-Day Plan to Reset Your Body* (New York: HarperOne, 2010), 14.

Page 156 *[He] would use several*: Frank Lewis Dyer and Thomas Commerford Martin, *Edison: His Life and Inventions* (New York: Harper and Brothers, 1910), 2:559.

Page 156 *[Napping] helps clear out*: Stickgold, "Simplest Way to Reboot."

Page 156 *Rosekind and his team*: Mark R. Rosekind et al., "Alertness Management: Strategic Naps in Operational Settings," *Journal of Sleep Research* 4, supplement 2 (1995): 62–66.

Page 157 *Take a Nap! Change Your Life*: Sara C. Mednick, *Take a Nap! Change Your Life* (New York: Workman, 2006), xv.

Page 157 *The effects of meditation*: Sara W. Lazar et al., "Functional Brain Mapping of the Relaxation Response and Meditation," *NeuroReport* 11, no. 7 (2000): 1581–85.

Page 158 *International Journal of Neuroscience*: Robert Keith Wallace et al., "The Effects of the Transcendental Meditation and TM-Sidhi Program on the Aging Process," *International Journal of Neuroscience* 16, no. 1 (1982): 53–58.

Page 158 *If we can affect*: Eva Selhub, personal communication with the authors, May 18, 2011.

Page 158 *Peace of mind sends*: Bernie S. Siegel, *Love, Medicine and Miracles: Lessons Learned about Self-Healing from a Surgeon's Experience with Exceptional Patients* (New York: Harper & Row, 1986), 3, 150.

Page 159 *The Relaxation Response*: Herbert Benson, *The Relaxation Response* (New York: Morrow, 1975).

Page 161 *Psychiatry Research: Neuroimaging*: Britta K. Hölzel et al., "Mindfulness Practice Leads to Increases in Regional Brain Gray Matter Density," *Psychiatry Research: Neuroimaging* 191, no. 1 (2011): 36–43.

Chapter 8: Liberate Your Mind by Synchronizing Your Brain

Page 164 *Technologies altering brainwave*: Michael Hutchison, *Megabrain: New Tools and Techniques for Brain Growth and Mind Expansion* (New York: Ballantine Books, 1996), 225–26.

Page 164 *Siegfried Othmer, PhD*: Jim Robbins, *A Symphony in the Brain: The Evolution of the New Brain Wave Biofeedback* (New York: Grove Press, 2008).

Page 167 *Auditory Beats in the Brain*: Gerald Oster, "Auditory Beats in the Brain," *Scientific American*, October 1973.

Page 167 *Research results show*: Michael Hutchison, personal communication with the authors, April 4, 1996. See also Hutchison, *Megabrain.*

Page 168 *training wheels for your brain*: Michael Hutchison, personal communication with the authors, April 4, 1996.

Page 170 *Subtle and ineffable*: "Behavior: Alpha Wave of the Future," *Time*, July 19, 1971, www.time.com/time/magazine/article /0,9171,905369,00.html. See also Les Fehmi and Jim Robbins, *The Open-Focus Brain: Harnessing the Power of Attention to Heal Mind and Body* (Boston: Trumpeter Books, 2007).

Page 170 *letting go of anxieties*: "Alpha Wave of the Future." See also Joe Kamiya, "Operant Control of the EEG Alpha Rhythm and Some of Its Reported Effects on Consciousness," in *Biofeedback and Self-Control: An Aldine Reader on the Regulation of Bodily Processes and Consciousness*, ed. Joe Kamiya et al. (Chicago: Aldine-Atherton, 1971).

Page 171 *Melinda Maxfield of the Foundation*: Melinda Maxfield, "The Journey of the Drum," *ReVision* 16, no. 4 (1994): 157.

Recommended Reading and Resources

We are grateful to all the researchers who are cited in the references section of this book, and we recommend that you explore their work in more depth. The resources we are recommending here are those that we believe will be most directly useful in helping you improve your mind as you age. The list is in alphabetical order, and we have limited ourselves to just one book recommendation from each author, although most are prolific writers and have authored many valuable works. We have provided the author's website (or other relevant website) when it was available. We also have included a number of websites useful for learning some of the skills introduced in the book. Web addresses listed below are all valid at the time of going to press.

Age Nation. http://agenation.com. Provides "information, inspiration and engagement" to those "committed to living vital, successful and conscious lives."

Agronin, Marc E. *How We Age: A Doctor's Journey into the Heart of Growing Old*. Cambridge, MA: Da Capo Press, 2011. Website: www.marc agronin.com.

Alexander Technique Workshops International. http://alexandertechnique workshops.com. Highly recommended seminars on the Alexander Technique.

Amen, Daniel G. *Magnificent Mind at Any Age: Natural Ways to Unleash Your Brain's Maximum Potential*. New York: Three Rivers Press, 2009. Website: www.amenclinics.com.

Barry, Dave. *Dave Barry Turns 40*. New York: Crown, 1990.

Benson, Herbert. *The Relaxation Response*. New York: Morrow, 1975. Website: www.relaxationresponse.org.

Bortz, Walter M., and Randall Stickrod. *The Roadmap to 100: The Breakthrough Science of Living a Long and Healthy Life*. New York: Palgrave Macmillan, 2010. Website: www.walterbortz.com.

Buettner, Dan. *The Blue Zones: Lessons for Living Longer from the People Who've Lived the Longest*. Washington, DC: National Geographic, 2008. Website: www.bluezones.com.

Buzan, Tony. *The Mind Map Book*. New York: Dutton, 1994. Website: www.thinkbuzan.com.

Cass, Hyla, and Patrick Holford. *Natural Highs: Supplements, Nutrition, and Mind-Body Techniques to Help You Feel Good All the Time*. New York: Avery, 2002. Website: www.cassmd.com.

Childre, Doc, and Howard Martin. *The HeartMath Solution: The Institute of HeartMath's Revolutionary Program for Engaging the Power of the Heart's Intelligence*. San Francisco: HarperSanFrancisco, 2000. Website: www.heartmath.org.

Chopra, Deepak, and David Simon. *Grow Younger, Live Longer: 10 Steps to Reverse Aging*. New York: Harmony Books, 2001. Website: www.chopra.com.

Cohen, Gene. *The Mature Mind: The Positive Power of the Aging Brain.* New York: Basic Books, 2006.

Damasio, Antonio. *Descartes' Error: Emotion, Reason, and the Human Brain.* New York: Putnam, 1994.

Diamond, Marian, and Janet Hopson. *Magic Trees of the Mind: How to Nurture Your Child's Intelligence, Creativity, and Healthy Emotions from Birth through Adolescence.* New York: Plume, 1999.

Doidge, Norman. *The Brain That Changes Itself: Stories of Personal Triumph from the Frontiers of Brain Science.* New York: Penguin, 2007. Website: www.normandoidge.com.

Dychtwald, Ken. *The Age Wave: How the Most Important Trend of Our Time Can Change Your Future.* New York: Bantam, 1990. Website: www .dychtwald.com.

Edlund, Matthew. *The Power of Rest: Why Sleep Alone Is Not Enough. A 30-Day Plan to Reset Your Body.* New York: HarperOne, 2010. Website: www.therestdoctor.com.

Emmons, Robert A., and Michael E. McCullough, eds. *The Psychology of Gratitude.* New York: Oxford University Press, 2004. Website: http://psychology.ucdavis.edu/labs/emmons/PWT/index.cfm.

Fehmi, Les, and Jim Robbins. *The Open-Focus Brain: Harnessing the Power of Attention to Heal Mind and Body.* Boston: Trumpeter Books, 2007. Website: www.openfocus.com.

Green, Elmer, and Alyce Green. *Beyond Biofeedback.* New York: Delacorte Press, 1977.

Gremillion, Valerie. Website: www.valeriegremillion.com.

Hutchison, Michael. *Megabrain: New Tools and Techniques for Brain Growth and Mind Expansion.* New York: Ballantine Books, 1996.

Iacoboni, Marco. *Mirroring People: The Science of Empathy and How We Connect with Others.* New York: Picador, 2009.

Kabat-Zinn, Jon. *Wherever You Go, There You Are: Mindfulness Meditation in Everyday Life.* New York: Hyperion, 1994. Website: www.mindfulness tapes.com.

Keene, Raymond. *Complete Book of Beginning Chess*. Las Vegas, NV: Cardoza, 2003. Website: www.keeneonchess.com.

Langer, Ellen J. *Counterclockwise: Mindful Health and the Power of Possibility*. New York: Ballantine Books, 2009. Website: www.ellenlanger.com.

Levy, Becca. Yale School of Public Health. http://medicine.yale.edu/ysph /people/becca_levy-3.profile. This webpage contains a list of Levy's publications.

Lipton, Bruce H. *The Biology of Belief: Unleashing the Power of Consciousness, Matter and Miracles*. Santa Rosa, CA: Elite Books, 2005. Website: www.brucelipton.com.

Luskin, Fred. *Forgive for Good: A Proven Prescription for Health and Happiness*. San Francisco: HarperSanFrancisco, 2003. Website: www.learningtoforgive.com.

Medina, John. *Brain Rules: 12 Principles for Surviving and Thriving at Work, Home, and School*. Seattle: Pear Press, 2008. Website: www .brainrules.net.

Merzenich, Michael. Posit Science. www.positscience.com. This website contains information on brain-training programs.

Pink, Daniel H. *A Whole New Mind: Why Right-Brainers Will Rule the Future*. New York: Riverhead Books, 2006. Website: www.danpink.com.

Ranck, Chris. *Ignite the Genius Within: Discover Your Full Potential*. New York: Plume, 2010. Website: www.christineranck.com.

Ratey, John J. *Spark: The Revolutionary New Science of Exercise and the Brain*. New York: Little, Brown, 2008. Website: www.johnratey.com.

Restak, Richard. *Mozart's Brain and the Fighter Pilot: Unleashing Your Brain's Potential*. New York: Three Rivers Press, 2002. Website: www.richard restak.com.

Robbins, Jim. *A Symphony in the Brain: The Evolution of the New Brain Wave Biofeedback*. New York: Grove Press, 2008.

Roizen, Michael F., and Mehmet C. Oz. *YOU: Staying Young; The Owner's Manual for Extending Your Warranty*. New York: Free Press, 2007. Website: www.realage.com.

Russell, Peter. *The Brain Book: Know Your Own Mind and How to Use It.* London: Routledge, 1994. Website: www.peterrussell.com.

Schwartz, Jeffrey M., and Sharon Begley. *The Mind and the Brain: Neuroplasticity and the Power of Mental Force.* New York: ReganBooks, 2002.

Sears, Al. *PACE: The 12-Minute Fitness Revolution.* Royal Palm Beach, FL: Wellness Research Foundation, 2010. Website: www.alsearsmd.com.

Selhub, Eva. *The Love Response: Your Prescription to Turn Off Fear, Anger, and Anxiety to Achieve Vibrant Health and Transform Your Life.* New York: Ballantine Books, 2009. Website: www.drselhub.com.

Seligman, Martin E. P. *Learned Optimism: How to Change Your Mind and Your Life.* New York: Pocket Books, 1998. Website: www.ppc.sas.upenn.edu.

Siegel, Bernie S. *Love, Medicine and Miracles: Lessons Learned about Self-Healing from a Surgeon's Experience with Exceptional Patients.* New York: HarperPerennial, 1990. Website: www.berniesiegelmd.com.

Tangora, Robert. *The Internal Structure of Cloud Hands.* Berkeley, CA: North Atlantic Books, forthcoming. Website: www.tangorataichi.com. Tangora's website offers instructional DVDs for learning tai chi.

Third Age. www.thirdage.com. A website devoted to the more than 112 million people over age forty-five in the United States.

Weil, Andrew. *Healthy Aging: A Lifelong Guide to Your Physical and Spiritual Well-Being.* New York: Knopf, 2005. Website: www.drweil.com.

Wiseman, Richard. www.richardwiseman.com.

Acknowledgments

Our deep gratitude goes to all who contributed to the creation of this book and inspired us along the way: Dr. Marc Agronin, Dr. Daniel Amen, Dave Barry, Sharon Begley, Michael Knox Beran, Dr. Walter M. Bortz, Dr. Hyla Cass, Dr. Deepak Chopra, Dr. Gene Cohen, Dr. Marian C. Diamond, Dr. Norman Doidge, Dr. Matthew Edlund, Dr. Les Fehmi, Dr. Bob Friedman, Sandy and Joan Gelb, Dr. George Gerbner, Dr. Vincent Giampapa, Dr. Valerie Gremillion, Dr. Tereza Hubkova, Michael Hutchison, Professor Marco Iacoboni, Byron Katie, Grandmaster Raymond Keene, Dr. Cynthia Kenyon, Dr. Midori Koga, Dr. Ellen J. Langer, Dr. Becca Levy, Dr. Bruce H. Lipton, Judith Martin, Dr. John Medina, Dr. Michael Merzenich, Marilyn Preston, Dr. John Ratey, Professor Mark R. Rosenzweig, Professor Mary J. Schleppegrell, Dr. Jeffrey M. Schwartz, Dr. Al Sears, Dr. Eva Selhub, Dr. Martin E. P.

Seligman, Dr. Norman Shealy, Professor Joe Verghese, and Dr. Andrew Weil.

We are also very grateful for the support and expertise provided by the superb team at New World Library: Jason Gardner, Kristen Cashman, Munro Magruder, Monique Muhlenkamp, Tona Pearce Myers, Tracy Cunningham, and copyeditor Mark Colucci.

Extra special thanks go to Tony Buzan, Deborah Domanski, and William Smythe.

Index

Blue Zones, The (Buettner), 140
Blumenthal, James A., 76
body/mind duality, 70–71
Bogart, Humphrey, 180
Bombeck, Erma, 32
bone density, 81
Bortz, Walter M., 69–70, 143–44, 152
BOSU balls, 85
Bouhours, Dominique, 181
Boyle, Patricia A., 43
brain
    cell reconstruction in, 92
    complexity of, 1, 6–7
    environment as influence on, 123, 125–26
    fat content of, 101
    improvement of, with use, 46, 47, 48–49, 66
    oxygenation of, 72, 90, 179
    physical exercise as influence on, 71
    rewiring of, from negative thought patterns, 18–20
    rustproofing, 92, 95–99, 109
    water content of, 93
    See also brain power; brain waves; environment, brain-enhancing
brain cells, generation of, in old age, 5
Brain Fitness Program, 57
"brain games," 62–63
brain power
    attitude and, 12–14
    examples of, 1–3
    juggling and, 63–65
    physical exercise as influence on, 71–72
    unleashing, 6–9, 179–80
    See also environment, brain-enhancing
Brain Rules (Medina), 71, 134
Brain Sync: Improve Your Mind as You Age (audio program), 8
    benefits of, 166, 175, 176–77
    FAQs, 174–77
    format of, 165

how it works, 166–68
listening instructions, 172–74
track 1 (*Introduction*), 165
track 2 (*Pure Coherence*), 165–66, 169, 172–73
track 3 (*Deep Resonance*), 165–66, 170, 172, 173
track 4 (*Slow-Wave Sleep*), 154, 165–66, 172, 173–74
Brain That Changes Itself, The (Doidge), 6
brain waves
    binaural frequencies, 166–68
    perfect, catching, 168
    training in, 163–64 (*see also Brain Sync: Improve Your Mind as You Age*)
    types of, 168–72
Brave New World (Huxley), 180
breakfast, 92, 121
breathing, 160
bridge (card game), 58, 63
Brillat-Savarin, Jean Anthelme, 113, 116
British Medical Journal, 88
Buettner, Dan, 140
Buffett, Warren, 42
Burns, George, 27, 39, 136
Buzan, Tony, 56, 139

C

Cacioppo, John T., 138, 139
caffeine, 94, 114, 153
calisthenics, 81
Calms Forté, 154
Canadian Journal of Human Sexuality, 148–49
cancer
    diet and, 97, 98, 103, 113, 116–17
    support groups for, 137
carbohydrates
    high-glycemic, 99, 103–4, 121
    low-glycemic, 104
cardiovascular functioning, 30

H

habits, 42
    breaking out of patterns, 46, 47
    forming of, 18
    negative, 18–19
Hackman, Gene, 24
happiness, 28, 66–67
Harvard Medical School, 89
Hay, Louise, 41
headaches, 94
Healing and the Mind (PBS TV series),
    160
Health and Light (Ott), 129
Healthy Aging (Weil), 60
hearing, 30, 126
heart attacks, 115
heartburn, 112, 126
heart disease
    diet and, 97, 98, 103, 115, 116–17
    exercise and resistance to, 69–70
    sleep and susceptibility to, 152
HeartMath Solution, The (Childre and
    Martin), 24
Hebb, Donald O., 18
Hemingway, Ernest, 30
herbs, 98
Herz-Sommer, Alice, 124
Hippocrates, 70, 71, 75, 95
hip replacements, 17
Hirschstein, Ami Jayaprada, 83
Holford, Patrick, 104
Holmes, Clive, 132
Hölzel, Britta K., 161
Hopper, Grace Murray, 40
Hopson, Janet, 134
Horace, 151
hormone replacement therapy (HRT),
    147
hormones, 128, 147
houseplants, 131
How to Live to Be 100 — or More
    (Burns), 39

How We Age (Agronin), 67
Hubkova, Tereza, 100
humor, 21, 26–28, 67, 179
Hutchinson, Michael, 167–68
Huxley, Aldous, 180
hydration, 92, 93–94, 121
Hyman, Mark, 107

I

Iacoboni, Marco, 7, 48
immune function
    diet and, 98, 110
    exercise and, 81
    sleep and, 152
    social networks and, 137–38
    sunlight and, 128
"In Defense of Memorization" (Beran),
    51–52
indigestion, 126
inertia, overcoming, 73
inflammation, 99, 115
insomnia, 114, 126
insulin resistance, 102
intelligence, 4, 5, 18, 164
International Journal of Neuroscience, 158
Interpretation of Dreams, The (Freud),
    152
In the Company of Animals (Serpell),
    141–42
IQ, 4, 5, 164

J

James, William, 11, 18, 28, 49, 123–24
Jean Paul, 78
Jeffers, Susan, 47
Jefferson, Thomas, 21, 36, 139
Johns Hopkins University, 133
Johnson, Lyndon B., 38
jokes, 27–28
Jonides, John, 130
Joudry, Patricia, 174

Longfellow, Henry Wadsworth, 25–26, 182
Loren, Sophia, 42–43
love, 38
Love, Medicine and Miracles (Siegel), 158–60
"Love Response," 142
Loving What Is (Katie), 20
Luskin, Fred, 24

M

MacArthur, Douglas, 19
MacDonald, Ian, 115
Magic Trees of the Mind (Diamond and Hopson), 134
Martin, Howard, 24
Martin, Judith, 148
Martin, Thomas, 156
Marx, Groucho, 181
Master Your Memory (Buzan), 56
mattress, choice of, 153
maturity, 39
Matzkin, Alice, 34
Matzkin, Richard, 34
Maugham, W. Somerset, 60, 163
Maxfield, Melinda, 171
Max Planck Institute for Human Development (Berlin, Germany), 66
Mayo Clinic, 110
McCartney, Paul, 85
McCullough, Michael E., 22
media, elderly as portrayed in, 33–34
Medical News Today, 63
Medina, John, 71, 134
meditation, 157–62, 163, 171–72, 174, 176
Meditations on First Philosophy (Descartes), 70–71
Mediterranean diet, 91, 103, 117
Mednick, Sara C., 157
Megabrain (Hutchinson), 167–68
melatonin, 153, 154
memorization, 51–53

memory
    diet as influence on, 94, 95, 108–9
    environment as influence on, 127
    faulty ideas about, 4, 69–70
    meditation and, 157–58
    napping and, 157
    negative thought patterns about, 20–21
    physical exercise as influence on, 71, 76–77
    skills for increasing, 4, 5
    tests, elder performance on, 30
    tips for increasing, 49–57
memory systems (mnemonics), 53–56, 65
mental capacity, 4
mental rest, 155
mental sports, 57–59, 65
mentoring, 140
Merriam-Webster word of the day, 63
Merzenich, Michael, 47, 57
metabolic disorders, 102
metabolism, 81, 128
metaphors, changing, 147–48
Michelangelo, 36
mind, improvement of, 3–5
mind/body duality, 70–71
mindfulness, 74–75, 91, 119–20, 121, 146–47
Mindfulness-Based Stress Reduction (MBSR) program, 161
Mind Map Book, The (Buzan), 56
Mind Maps, 56
mineral supplements, 107
Miss Manners' Guide to Excruciatingly Correct Behavior (Martin), 148
Mizner, Wilson, 141
mnemonics, 53–56, 65
moderation, 92, 102, 112–17
modern lifestyle, 130–31
monosodium glutamate (MSG), 105–6
mood disorders, 102, 109, 126, 157
    See also depression
Moore, Hannah, 23

pharmaceuticals, 109, 112
phosphatidylserine, 110
physical rest, 155
Pilates, 90
planned obsolescence, 32
Plato, 70, 75, 133
Plutarch, 60
Pocket Idiot's Guide to 108 Yoga Poses (Hirschstein), 83
poetry, 66
poise, 83–84, 85–89
Pollan, Michael, 105
Pope, Alexander, 23
Pradervand, Pierre, 26
prescription drugs. *See* pharmaceuticals
present moment, living in, 146–47
preservatives, 97, 99, 105, 121
probiotics, 109–10
problem-solving skills, 77, 157
Proceedings of the National Academy of Sciences, 57
processed foods, 99, 105
protein, 95
Psychiatry Research: Neuroimaging, 161
Psychological Science, 130
Psychology and Aging, 62
Pugh, Emerson, 7
puns, 28
purpose, sense of, 43, 67

Q

quiet, 153

R

Ratey, John J., 71, 72
Rauscher, Frances H., 127–28
reading, 58, 62
relationships, healthy
    benefits of, 135–38, 142
    "Love Response" and, 142
    with pets, 141–42
    sexual, 143–49

as social wealth, 138–39, 179
    tips for cultivating, 139–41
"Relaxation Response," 159–60
Relaxation Response, The (Benson), 159
Renoir, Pierre August, 180
Research Project on Gratitude and Thankfulness, 22
resentment, 24, 26
resilience, 15
rest
    benefits of, 151, 162
    deprivation of, 155
    meditation, 157–62
    napping, 156–57
    sleep, 152–54
    types of, 155
Restak, Richard, 5, 46, 125
retirement, 30, 35, 138–39
revenge, forgiveness as, 25
Richter, Johann Paul Friedrich, 78
Ridley, Matt, 9
rigidity, 82
rituals, for sleeping well, 154
Roadmap to 100, The (Bortz), 69
Roizen, Michael F., 106, 118
Rosekind, Mark R., 156–57
Rosenzweig, Mark R., 125
Rosetta Stone language-learning software, 61–62
Royal Academy of Dramatic Arts, 85
running, 76, 77, 90
Rush University Alzheimer's Disease Center, 137

S

sauerkraut, 110
schedules, for sleeping well, 154
Schleppegrell, Mary J., 61
Schwartz, Jeffrey M., 19
Schweitzer, Albert, 21
Scrabble, 62, 63
Sears, Al, 79, 81
Seattle (Duwamish chief), 141

theta brain waves, 167, 170–72, 173
Thoreau, Henry David, 118, 131
Three Minutes in Heaven (erotic game), 145–46
Time magazine, 39
Tomiyama, Janet A., 119
toothbrushing, 117–18
tooth decay, 117
Transcendental Meditation, 158
trans fat, 99, 102, 121
Tubman, Harriet, 37–38
turmeric, 111

U

ulcers, 94, 117, 126
UltraMind Solution, The (Hyman), 107
Unforgiven, The (film; 1992), 24–25
unintentional chronic dehydration (UCD), 94
United States, negative aging stereotypes in, 28–29, 31–32, 33–34
United States Weight Control Registry, 94–95
University of Copenhagen (Denmark), 121
University of Massachusetts Medical Center, 160
University of Toronto (Canada), 95
University of Vienna (Austria), 113–14

V

valerian, 154
Vanderbilt University Institute for Coffee Studies, 114–15
vegetables, 97, 104, 109
Verghese, Joe, 58
Vikan, Gary, 133
Vinson, Joe, 114
Virginia Technical University, 110
vitamin C, 108
Vitamin C and the Common Cold (Pauling), 108

vitamin D, 107–8
vitamin E, 98
vocabulary, upgrading, 62–63, 65
Voltaire, 118
volunteering, 140
vulnerability, 148–49

W

Walker, Thomas, 117
walking, 76–77, 90
    curb walking (balance exercise), 84–85
Wallace, Robert Keith, 158
Walters Art Museum (Baltimore, MD), 133
warm-ups, before exercising, 73, 82
Watson, James D., 1
Wayne, Peter M., 89
web-savviness, 66
weight control, 94–95, 118–19
weight gain, 104
Weil, Andrew, 60
When Bad Things Happen to Good People (Kushner), 23
whining, 2–3, 35, 140
"Why I'd Rather Sleep with an Old Guy" (Forsythe), 149
Wilde, Oscar, 25, 181
wine, red, 91, 115, 116–17
Wine Spectator (magazine), 116, 117
wisdom
    age as price of, 11
    happiness and, 66–67
Wiseman, Richard, 27
Wolf, Steven L., 89–90
Wooden, John, 40–41
Woodward, Joanne, 145
word-of-the-day services, 63
Wordsworth, William, 129
"Work, the," 20
worry, 18, 160
Wright, Steven, 153
writing, 65–66

Y

Yalow, Rosalyn, 41
Yeh, Gloria, 89
yoga, 82–83, 90
yogurt, 110
You Can Heal Your Life (Hay), 41
Young, Michael, 146

Your Body's Many Cries for Water (Batmanghelidj), 94
YOU: Staying Young (Roizen and Oz), 118

Z

"zone, the," 173

About the Authors

Michael J. Gelb is the world's leading authority on the application of genius thinking to personal and organizational development. He is a pioneer in the fields of creative thinking, accelerated learning, and innovative leadership. Michael leads seminars for organizations such as DuPont, Merck, Microsoft, Nike, Raytheon, and YPO. He brings more than thirty years of experience as a professional speaker, seminar leader, and organizational consultant to his diverse, international clientele.

Michael is the author of twelve books on accelerated learning, creativity, and innovation, including the international bestseller *How to Think Like Leonardo da Vinci: Seven Steps to Genius Every Day* (1998). *How to Think Like*

Leonardo da Vinci has been translated into twenty-five languages and has appeared on the *Washington Post*, Amazon .com, and *New York Times* bestseller lists.

In 2007, Michael released *Innovate Like Edison: The Success System of America's Greatest Inventor*, coauthored with Sarah Miller Caldicott, the great-grandniece of Thomas Edison. As Professor Vijay Govindarajan, author of *Ten Rules for Strategic Innovators*, noted, "This book is a must-have for anyone who wants to turn creative ideas into profitable reality."

In 1999, Michael won the Brain Trust Charity's "Brain of the Year" award; other honorees include Stephen Hawking, Bill Gates, Garry Kasparov, and Gene Roddenberry. In 2003, Michael was awarded a Batten Fellowship by the University of Virginia's Darden Graduate School of Business. Michael codirects the acclaimed Leading Innovation Seminar at Darden with Professor James Clawson. Michael also serves as the director of creativity and innovation leadership for the Conscious Capitalism Institute.

A former professional juggler who once performed with the Rolling Stones and Bob Dylan, Michael introduced the idea of teaching juggling as a means of promoting accelerated learning and team building. He is the author of *Five Keys to High Performance: Juggle Your Way to Success*. A fourth-degree black belt in the Japanese martial art of aikido, Michael is coauthor, with international grandmaster Raymond Keene, of *Samurai Chess: Mastering Strategic Thinking through the Martial Art of the Mind*. Michael is also a certified teacher of the Alexander technique (the method taught at the Juilliard School for cultivating a commanding stage presence) and the author of the classic work *Body Learning:*

An Introduction to the Alexander Technique. Michael's 1988 release *Present Yourself! Captivate Your Audience with Great Presentation Skills* guides readers to develop the communication strategies they need to generate support for their innovative ideas.

Michael has also created many bestselling audio programs, including *Mind Mapping: How to Liberate Your Natural Genius*, *Work Like da Vinci: Gaining the Creative Advantage in Your Business and Career*, and *The Spirit of Leonardo*.

Michael's passion for applying genius thinking to personal and organizational development is also expressed in his 2003 HarperCollins release *Discover Your Genius: How to Think Like History's Ten Most Revolutionary Minds*.

A devoted aficionado of fine wine, Michael is the author of *Wine Drinking for Inspired Thinking: Uncork Your Creative Juices*, a book that offers a unique, original, and very enjoyable approach to team building as well as useful practical advice on how to buy, store, serve, and enjoy the "elixir of genius."

Michael has been researching, teaching, and applying the principles of brain optimization throughout his career, but after thirty years, he muses, "Now, it's serious!"

His website is www.michaelgelb.com.

Kelly Howell, creator of Brain Sync, is the world's leading authority on brain wave audio technology. With almost three million audio programs in circulation and decades of experience, Kelly is renowned for her revolutionary work in meditation and mind expansion. Her visionary recording techniques have helped hundreds of thousands of individuals achieve personal and professional goals, experience more peaceful states of mind, and enhance their mental performance.

In the early 1980s, Kelly authored dozens of highly popular self-help programs, including one of the bestselling audio programs of all time, *Slim Forever*. Having become fascinated with brain wave altering techniques, she went on to create a superb series of brain optimization programs called Super Mind, published by Random House.

As an early pioneer in the practical application of brain wave research, Kelly was commissioned by eminent doctors and neuroscientists to create clinical programs for the treatment of depression, insomnia, and addiction. Today, Kelly's life-changing audio programs are used in biofeedback clinics, hospitals, and wellness centers worldwide.

Kelly is also host of the much-loved *Theatre of the Mind* podcast and radio show, which explores mind expansion, creativity, and the many facets of human potential.

In an age when life is becoming exceedingly hectic, Kelly's guidance and instruction are invaluable. She is affectionately called the "brain whisperer" by her many fans.

Her website is www.brainsync.com.

JAICO PUBLISHING HOUSE
Elevate Your Life. Transform Your World.

ESTABLISHED IN 1946, Jaico Publishing House is home to world-transforming authors such as Sri Sri Paramahansa Yogananda, Osho, The Dalai Lama, Sri Sri Ravi Shankar, Sadhguru, Robin Sharma, Deepak Chopra, Jack Canfield, Eknath Easwaran, Devdutt Pattanaik, Khushwant Singh, John Maxwell, Brian Tracy and Stephen Hawking.

Our late founder Mr. Jaman Shah first established Jaico as a book distribution company. Sensing that independence was around the corner, he aptly named his company Jaico ('Jai' means victory in Hindi). In order to service the significant demand for affordable books in a developing nation, Mr. Shah initiated Jaico's own publications. Jaico was India's first publisher of paperback books in the English language.

While self-help, religion and philosophy, mind/body/spirit, and business titles form the cornerstone of our non-fiction list, we publish an exciting range of travel, current affairs, biography, and popular science books as well. Our renewed focus on popular fiction is evident in our new titles by a host of fresh young talent from India and abroad. Jaico's recently established Translations Division translates selected English content into nine regional languages.

In addition to being a publisher and distributor of its own titles, Jaico is a major national distributor of books of leading international and Indian publishers. With its headquarters in Mumbai, Jaico has branches and sales offices in Ahmedabad, Bangalore, Bhopal, Bhubaneswar, Chennai, Delhi, Hyderabad, Kolkata and Lucknow.

SINCE 1946